THE REAL
JOAQUIN MURIETA

Robin Hood Hero or Gold Rush Gangster?

by REMI NADEAU

Also by Remi Nadeau:

City-Makers
The Water-Seekers
Los Angeles: From Mission to Modern City
California: The New Society
Ghost Towns and Mining Camps of California
Fort Laramie and the Sioux Indians

THE REAL
JOAQUIN MURIETA

Robin Hood Hero or Gold Rush Gangster?

by REMI NADEAU

TRANS-ANGLO BOOKS

The *Real* Joaquin Murieta

Copyright © MCMLXXIV by Remi Nadeau

FIRST EDITION

Library of Congress Catalog Card No.: 73:87362

ISBN: 0-87046-027-7

Frontispiece: This painting, in The Press Club of San Francisco (formerly The Union League Club), depicts an idealized Joaquin Murieta riding his horse on a sheer Sierra ledge during an infamous raid. The painter was Charles Christian Nahl (1818-78). (Photograph by Ken Arnold)

Other Illustrations: Uncredited half-page drawings in this volume, except as noted, originally appeared in the 1859 serialization of Joaquin Murieta's life in The California Police Gazette.

Endsheets — Front: View of the Sierra foothills from the cemetery at Hornitos, photographed by Victoria Crump. Back: The forested Sierra country where Joaquin Murieta eluded pursuers, photographed by John Crump.

Printed and Bound in the United States of America

A Spencer Crump Publication: Published by Trans-Anglo Books
P. O. Box 38, Corona del Mar, California 92625

4

To Christine, Barbara, Roland and Remi Robert

WILL BE EXHIBITED

FOR ONE DAY ONLY!

AT THE STOCKTON HOUSE!

THIS DAY, AUG. 12, FROM 9 A. M., UNTIL 6, P. M.

THE HEAD

Of the renowned Bandit!

JOAQUIN!

AND THE

HAND OF THREE FINGERED JACK!

THE NOTORIOUS ROBBER AND MURDERER.

"JOAQUIN" and "THREE-FINGERED JACK" were captured by the *State Rangers*, under the command of Capt. Harry Love, at the Arroya Cantina, July 24th. No reasonable doubt can be entertained in regard to the identification of the head now on exhibition, as being that of the notorious robber, *Joaquin Murietta*, as it has been recognised by hundreds of persons who have formerly seen him.

Table of Contents

Left: This 1853 broadside advertised an exhibition of the pur-ported head of Joaquin Murieta and the hand of his alleged companion, Three-fingered Jack. Joaquin's legend was only be-ginning to unfold.

Foreword

Some people believe it is a spoilsport business to dissect a legend and try to pick out the truth. Certainly legends have a wonderful entertainment value, but the quest to find out what really happened can be even more exciting.

Of course, one man's legend can be another man's fact. It depends largely on the historical methods used, together with the degree of one's skepticism versus the degree of one's desire to believe.

This book is an attempt to approach the Joaquin saga with the research and analysis that I believe are generally accepted among historians. It is an effort to establish all that really happened of which we have proof, or at least the highest probability, from contemporary sources that have so far come to light. It is also an effort to identify those things which never happened, but are only the product of fancy.

Between these two extremes lies an intriguing gray area of possible truth, which may be narrowed still further as new facts are uncovered in the irresistible story of Joaquin.

My own labors in this vineyard started in January 1958, when I began research on a Joaquin article for *Westways*. To my delight my first foray resulted in finding a profusion of contemporary news reports about Joaquin in the Stockton *San Joaquin Republican,* January to August, 1853. The extent of my research off and on over the next fifteen years is indicated in the bibliography at the back of this book. Along the way I was aided by a number of people, who are identified below in the positions they occupied at the time.

James R. Koping, Supervising Reference Librarian, Stockton Public Library.

Allan R. Ottley, Librarian, California Section, The California State Library, Sacramento.

John Barr Tompkins, Head of Public Services, The Bancroft Library, University of California, Berkeley.

W. N. Davis, Jr., Chief of Archives, and George A. Hruneni, Archivist, California State Archives, Sacramento.

Marcus A. McCorison, Librarian, American Antiquarian Society, Worcester, Massachusetts.

Frederick L. Arnold, Reference and Interlibrary Loan Librarian, Princeton University Library, Princeton, New Jersey.

William B. Secrest, Saga-West Publishing Company, Fresno.

Richard H. Dillon, Librarian, Sutro Library, San Francisco

Dr. Raymund F. Wood, School of Library Service, University of California at Los Angeles.

Donald Segerstrom, Sonora, California.

In addition to the libraries cited above, the following were also sources of information:

Henry E. Huntington Library and Art Gallery, San Marino

Los Angeles Public Library

San Diego Public Library

Stanford University Library

Lastly, I wish to thank my wife, Margaret, for her important contribution to the research for this book.

CHAPTER ONE

Joaquin—Myth and Counter Myth

O N JULY 25, 1853, a small party of American frontiers-men headed by one Harry Love rode into a camp of Mexicans on the west edge of California's San Joaquin Valley. With a commission from the state legislature, Captain Love and

Left: This drawing from a series on Joaquin Murieta's life published in the 1850s epitomized his daring. Jumping onto a table in a saloon, he dared onlookers. The illustration's contemporary lines were: "I am Joaquin! I dare you to shoot!" (California State Library)

11

his men were hunting the bandit Joaquin, who had terrorized the gold mines for two months in the previous winter.

Accosted by the intruders, the Mexican leader leaped on his horse and fled. The Americans fired at him and his companions. After a half-hour running battle, four Mexicans lay dead, including their chief.

To prove they were entitled to the reward money, the Americans cut off the leader's head. For good measure they cut off the deformed hand of another they identified as Three-fingered Jack. When these were exhibited back at the settlements, 16 persons signed affidavits that this was, in fact, the head of the celebrated bandit, Joaquin Murieta. Harry Love and his men split the $1000 reward money, and Love himself received an additional $5000 from the legislature.

So ended the saga of Joaquin, whose gang had killed more people than any other California outlaw, before or since.

But the legend of Joaquin was just beginning to unfold. The following year a young San Francisco journalist, John Rollin Ridge, wrote *The Life and Adventures of Joaquin Murieta*. A ninety-page paperback, it offered a vivid biography full of incidents that had never been reported before.

It told of savage injustices — the lynching of Joaquin's brother on a trumped-up charge, the ravishing of his sweetheart — that had sent Joaquin on a career of revenge.

It told of his sweetheart's travels with the gang on adventures throughout the state for three years. It related the bloodthirsty antics of the cutthroat, Three-fingered Jack, whose revolting crimes Joaquin tried and failed to curb. It gave detailed conversations between Joaquin and his men, as though the author had sat at their campfires with a notebook. It pictured Joaquin as a romantic avenger, the champion of a downtrodden people, a potential Mexican revolutionist in California.

John Rollin Ridge (left) was the young journalist whose 1854 biography of Joaquin Murieta spurred interest in the outlaw.

13

Ridge wrote, in short, in the tradition of the legendmakers of King Arthur and Robin Hood, of Roland and El Cid. But to authenticate his own story, Ridge introduced it with a remarkable statement of self-contradiction: "In the main, it will be found to be strictly true."

Though *The Life and Adventures of Joaquin Murieta* received only moderate attention, it crystalized the bandit's career in the minds of Californians. Because Ridge had chronicled them in rich and unequivocal detail, previously unsolved crimes throughout the state in the early 1850s were now definitely attributed to Joaquin.

From this time on the Ridge biography, rather than the contemporary newspaper accounts during Joaquin's life, became the accepted version of the robber's history. In 1858 it went on the San Francisco stage in a five-act drama, *Joaquin Murieta de Castillo,* which made the bandit into a Spaniard. In 1859 the *California Police Gazette* magazine began serializing "The Life of Joaquin Murieta, Brigand Chief of California," and then compiled it in a paperback book. Other than giving Joaquin two sweethearts instead of one, and providing still more colorful detail, this version was similar to Ridge's.

But the *Police Gazette* story had the advantage of far wider circulation. The farther it traveled from California, where it was handicapped by the facts, the more Joaquin was welcomed as a folk hero of Wagnerian proportions. As early as 1854 one Eastern editor had predicted with tongue in cheek that Guiseppe Verdi "will make this man the tenor hero of some clamorous opera."

He could scarcely foresee that Joaquin's story would, in fact, be retold in biographies, novels and plays in Spain, France, Chile and Mexico — most of them changing his nationality to suit their readers; that it would be canonized by the two principal California historians of the 19th Century — Hubert Howe Bancroft and Theodore Hittell; that it would be retold in newspaper "reminiscences" for the next half-century; that it would be sung in an epic poem that would give to its author the name of "Joaquin" Miller; that it would generate through much of

14

Northern California legendary "haunts" of Joaquin Murieta and tales of his buried treasure; and finally that it would achieve the ultimate romanticization in a Class A Hollywood motion picture, *The Robin Hood of El Dorado,* with more dramatic impact than a Verdi opera.

Joaquin had taken his place among the giant rogues of history. Now it was Robin Hood, Dick Turpin, Jesse James, *and* Joaquin Murieta.

In 1932 Francis P. Farquhar, editing a reprint of the *Police Gazette* version, demonstrated how it had been pirated from John Rollin Ridge, and went on to uncover later piratings of piratings. In 1939 Franklin P. Walker, in his *San Francisco's Literary Frontier,* speculated that much of the blood-and-thunder in Ridge's *The Life and Adventures of Joaquin Murieta* was invented by an imaginative author with a paranoid sympathy for underdogs.

Then beginning in 1941 Joseph Henry Jackson applied exhaustive literary detective work in his book *Anybody's Gold* and in later writings. He not only exposed the whole chain of myths from Ridge to Hollywood, but showed that contemporary editors of 1853 had attacked Harry Love's "head of Joaquin" as a humbug.

But Jackson went still further. Having helped to demolish all the Murieta biographies, he concluded that, ergo, "there wasn't a Murieta — at any rate not much of a Murieta . . ." And finally, "It is not too much to say that Ridge, in his preposterous little

*   *   *   *

Illustration Pages Following: This early-day map shows Calaveras County, where Joaquin Murieta centered many activities. The arrow points to the county's location in California. (University of California at Los Angeles Collection)

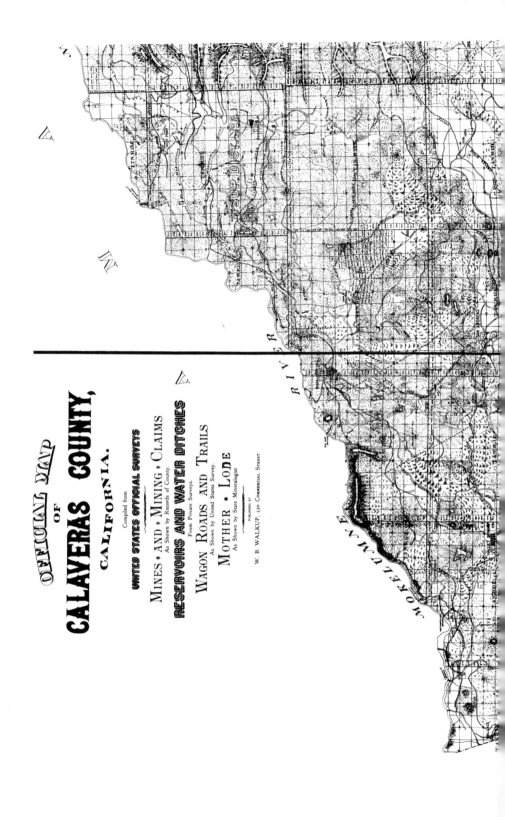

OFFICIAL MAP

OF

CALAVERAS COUNTY,

CALIFORNIA.

Compiled from

UNITED STATES OFFICIAL SURVEYS

MINES * AND * MINING * CLAIMS

As Shown by Records of County.

RESERVOIRS AND WATER DITCHES

From Private Surveys.

WAGON ROADS AND TRAILS

As Shown by United States Survey.

MOTHER * LODE

As Shown by State Mineralogist

PUBLISHED BY

W. B. WALKUP, 530 Commercial Street

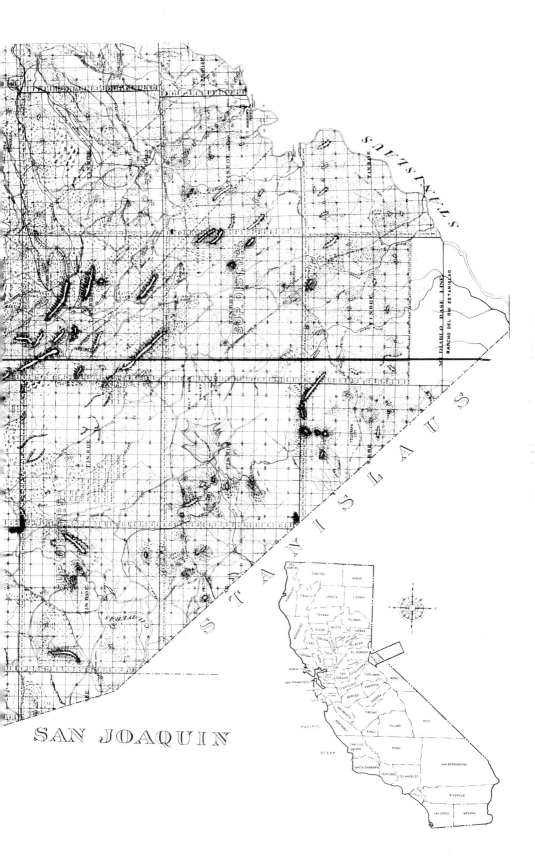

SAN JOAQUIN

book, actually created both the man, Murieta, and the Murieta legend as these stand today."

Myths die hard, as the scholars who unraveled the Arthurian legends and the tales of Robin Hood discovered. But at least the Murieta fictions had been exposed for those who cared to know the truth. And erudite readers of Californiana now believed a new myth — that Joaquin himself was fiction. The pendulum had swung to the other extreme.

The debunkers had conscientiously and correctly buried Joaquin the legend, but they had not dug anew for Joaquin the man. By exposing fiction they hardly proved there were no facts. Was there, then, a Joaquin?

For more than a half-century after Harry Love came out of San Joaquin Valley with what he called Joaquin's head, people came forward to claim they had known Joaquin. But most of their stories recounted circumstances and places otherwise mentioned only in the spurious Murieta biographies. They remind us of other literary efforts throughout history to attach one's self to an epic figure.

Though often useful in supplementing first-hand contemporary accounts, reminiscences are dubious as building blocks of history. The Joaquin reminiscences, in general, are further suspect because they link themselves with the legends that have since proven baseless. It is possible to construct a biography of Joaquin based on such reminiscences, but the cautious and healthy skepticism which should rule any historical research — and especially a story so liable to romanticizing — direct us more to other sources. The unvarnished truth is best served by sources contemporary with the actual event — diaries, letters, newspapers, legal records. These offer the best chance of isolating the real Joaquin.

Left: This sketch of Joaquin fleeing pursuers in the rugged Sierra country appeared as an illustration in John Rollin Ridge's original account of the outlaw's career.

19

In the two months of his documented career, Joaquin was a fleeting figure, striking here, being pursued there, surrounded but escaping elsewhere. A search of diaries and letters by Gold Rush pioneers yields no references to Joaquin as an acquaintance. Since the bandit was never captured and never tried for any offense, legal records have little reference to his life, although much to his final pursuit and supposed death.

The nature of Joaquin's life story points to newspapers as the best hunting ground, yet the one newspaper published in the heart of the supposed Murieta country, the Mokelumne Hill *Calaveras Chronicle,* has left practically no files for the year 1853 and earlier. Historical sleuthing, however, discloses the existence of files from other newspapers which maintained correspondents in the mines and reprinted articles from the *Calaveras Chronicle.* These include the San Francisco *Herald,* San Francisco *Alta California,* Sacramento *Union,* and most especially the Stockton *San Joaquin Republican.* Two files of mining town newspapers, the Columbia *Gazette* and the Auburn *Placer Herald,* are also rewarding.

From these sources, which often provide two or three supporting reports of the same episode, there emerges a Joaquin who terrorized Amador, Calaveras, and probably Mariposa counties for just two months — January to early March, 1853. In that short period he ran up such a fearful catalogue of crime that the local population began to flee and the Legislature was forced by aroused opinion to raise a company against him. Altogether, he and his band committed at least 24 and possibly 29 murders — a monstrous record.

There was, indeed, a Joaquin. Just as the literary scholars exposed the fictitious Joaquin, the following pages chronicle the real Joaquin.

Chapter Two

Prelude in Los Angeles

I N THE fall of 1851 Joaquin Murieta and his men stole 29 horses east of Los Angeles and drove them north. With their Mexican owner in pursuit, they traveled as far as Tejon Pass, which was then unguarded by soldiers, since Fort Tejon was not founded until three years later. But the local Tejon Indians stopped Joaquin and took some of the horses. Others were recovered by the owner, and Joaquin had failed in his first recorded crime.

Curiously, this episode is not mentioned by biographer Ridge, even though it appeared in two contemporary newspapers. But it was later picked up and elaborated by Major Horace Bell in his 1881 memoirs, *Reminiscences of a Ranger*. Though Bell did not arrive in Los Angeles until a year after the event, he described how the chief of the Tejons had Joaquin's party stripped naked, bound up, and thoroughly whipped before releasing them. The story was later embellished still further by Walter Noble Burns in his *Robin Hood of El Dorado.*

Actually, the incident proved that Joaquin was hardly a Mexican Robin Hood, since he had robbed one of his own compatriots. The crime is also one of the best authenticated of Joaquin's whole catalogue, since it was the only ever described in public testimony — and by one of his own gang, at that.

The occasion for the confession was a murder case in Los Angeles a year later in which Murieta's name was implicated. The testimony also revealed indirectly that Joaquin was a native of the Mexican state of Sonora, thus substantiating at least this much stated in his early biographies. More specifically, one of his followers (said by a later source to be Joaquin's nephew) testified that he himself was from the southern Sonora mining town of Bayoreca, located some 100 kilometers northwest of Alamos. If this was Joaquin's birthplace no record remains today, for Bayoreca is little more than a pile of rubble. But when Joaquin was a youngster it was a thriving silver town with a splendid church, a beautiful plaza, and a population of 1400.

Other leads on Joaquin's origins elsewhere in Sonora came forward many years later from persons claiming to be collateral descendants. But efforts to search church baptisms and other records have so far yielded no public proof of his Sonoran birthplace.

At any rate, by the time of the California gold discovery in 1848 the Sonora silver mines were in decline and hundreds of ore-wise Sonorans trekked northward to the new excitement. In fact, Los Angeles became a mecca for Sonorans in the 1850s. It then had little more than 1000 people, mostly Spanish-speaking. A number of Yankees had arrived during the Mexican Republic, and in the 1850s some of the more prosperous built two-story brick commercial buildings that stood in odd contrast to the prevailing one-story adobes of the essentially Spanish town.

During these developments the old district north of the plaza was given over largely to immigrants from Sonora, and hence earned the name of Sonoratown. In the 1850s it became both a halfway point for Sonorans on their way to the gold fields and a gathering place for others seeking jobs in Southern California's booming cattle business.

The Los Angeles in which Joaquin found himself in the early 1850s was hardly conducive to the peaceful life. Crossroads of the American and Spanish-Mexican frontiers, the city of the Angels had for years been the acknowledged hellhole of California. The 1849 Gold Rush to the north had created such a demand for beef that California's cattle trade boomed throughout the early 1850s. Money was plentiful in the southern pueblo, and as one arrival wrote in '49, "Gambling, drinking and whoring are the only occupation . . ." Such lush pickings naturally attracted scoundrels from the entire southwest, particularly when the vigilante movement of 1851 drove many of them out of Northern California. Horse stealing and highway robbery were rampant; as for murder, the editor of a Los Angeles weekly reported in the early '50s, "Four persons have been killed it is true, but it has been considered a poor week for killing."

To such a reckless atmosphere Joaquin and his countrymen took naturally. They were the heirs in the New World of the Spanish heroic tradition. In this mentality, each man was a dashing caballero, ready to rescue womanhood from everyone but himself, equally ready to defend his own honor against even a fancied slight or innuendo. Intrigue, bombast, bravado, physical prowess, a debonair and devil-may-care demeanor — these were a young man's hallmarks. Superb horsemanship was above all the requirement for good standing among one's peers.

Such Californians — native or immigrant — cut a colorful swath in early Los Angeles. From their hard-brimmed hats and their serapes to their button-sided trousers and heavyroweled spurs, they were dressed for heroic roles.

Sometimes this meant sheer banditry under the masquerade of guerrilla resistance to the Yankees. The principal gang then terrorizing Southern California was led by Solomon Pico, a

23

renegade from the distinguished Pico family that had produced California's last Mexican governor. Solomon's band, composed of native Californians and Sonorans, may have been joined for a time by Joaquin, as one public witness indicated.

Compounding the violent life were the Paiute Indians of the Mojave Desert, who had periodically crossed the Sierra Madre since the 1840s to raid Southern California ranches and run off with horses. To curb these forays the Angelenos in 1851 called upon Major General Joshua H. Bean, of the California state militia. The general was a former mayor of San Diego and a brother of the Roy Bean who, as Justice of the Peace in Langtry, Texas, would later call himself the "Law West of the Pecos."

Within a few months General Bean purged Los Angeles County of Indian raiders. Then he settled at San Gabriel, where he operated a store and saloon.

On the night of Sunday, November 7, 1852, Joaquin Murieta was in San Gabriel attending the *Maromas,* a performance featuring rope-dancing. With him was his paramour, Ana Benitez, a 22-year-old woman who had come to Los Angeles from Santa Fe, New Mexico. Ana Benitez — and not Rosita, Carmela, and others cited in the Joaquin biographies — was the only woman connected with Joaquin in the contemporary records. Her relationship with Joaquin is well established, since she herself later testified that Joaquin slept with her at the house of Juan Rico on the night of the *Maromas* in San Gabriel. Moreover, a member of Solomon Pico's band also testified: "I knew that Ana belonged to the gang of robbers, because she herself told me that she was the woman of Joaquin."

Also attending the *Maromas* was General Joshua Bean. Apparently one of the last to leave, he was approaching his lodging in San Gabriel when he was ambushed in the dark and shot through the chest. Drawing his revolver, the indomitable Indian fighter fired three random shots. Then he stumbled on (acording to Ana's testimony), calling "Rico! Rico! Rico!" One of Juan Rico's sons ran out and helped him to the house where Ana and her lover were staying. Señora Rico opened the door.

"Mother," panted the boy, holding the victim in his arms, "It is General Bean."

24

According to Ana, Joaquin himself ran out to get the local authorities. Three doctors arrived to shoulder their way through the crowd that had formed. Bean died late the following night.

The assassination was too much for the long-suffering Angelenos. Scarcely had they attended the General's funeral — the city's largest up to that time — than they began rounding up suspects on November 25. They brought in seven native Californians and Sonorans, but Joaquin himself was nowhere to be found. Impatient with legal processes, they formed a vigilance committee to examine the prisoners in a small, two-room adobe on Main Street.

Among those arrested was Ana Benitez, who swore that Joaquin Murieta had been with her at the time of the shooting. But a young Sonoran, Reyes Feliz, testified that according to a conversation he had overheard between some men, "Murieta's woman had said that Joaquin Murieta had killed him." Another witness, Benito Lopez of Solomon Pico's gang, swore that when he went to see Ana the night Bean was shot, it was not Joaquin but another man whe was with her.

"She told me that Joaquin had gone to the Tulares [San Joaquin Valley] to sell about 30 horses that he had stolen . . ."

But Ana not only persisted in her story, she also accused one Cipriano Sandoval, a native Californian who was the village cobbler at San Gabriel. The day after the shooting, she said, Joaquin was riding with her to Los Angeles. Near Mission San Gabriel they were overtaken by Sandoval, who was carrying a revolver in his waistband.

"Hombre," he supposedly said to Joaquin, "I charge you to keep the secret of what I have done."

When they had left him, recalled Ana, Murieta told her that Sandoval had killed Bean, and warned her against telling anyone.

Immediately Sandoval was arrested, and denied everything. Reyes Feliz, a lad of 15 or 16, proclaimed his innocence, but made the mistake of admitting that he had killed another person in Sonoratown, that he "belonged to the company of Joaquin Murieta," and that they had stolen horses.

25

Next day, November 27, a huge crowd at the adobe courthouse voted to hang Reyes Feliz — not because he had killed General Bean, but because he was a bad *hombre,* anyway. Young Feliz was hustled to a nearby hill and hanged on an improvised gallows.

Shortly afterward Cipriano Sandoval changed his story before the citizens' committee and swore that Felipe Read, a halfbreed son of the early Scottish settler, Hugo Read, had confessed the crime to him. Read was also arrested and examined, but was set free. Apparently believing the story by Murieta's woman, the vigilantes voted to hang Sandoval. In their fury they also condemned Benito Lopez, who had nothing to do with Bean's death, but had confessed to two other murders. Hanged with these two on December 4 was another who was not even dignified by having his name reported in the Los Angeles newspaper.

For years the horror of these public murders preyed upon the minds of sober Angelenos. District Judge Benjamin Hayes, whose court had been sidetracked by Judge Lynch, analyzed the evidence and wrote in his scrapbook that he believed Sandoval was innocent. Whether he suspected Felipe Read or Joaquin Murieta is not clear.

Anxious to build his tale of horror, John Rollin Ridge vividly described how Joaquin and Three-fingered Jack had killed General Bean. Other biographers followed suit. More conservative (for once), Walter Noble Burns wrote that "either Murieta directed the crime or was himself the assassin." Horace Bell flatly lays the murder at the door of Felipe Read. The public record shows only that through the year 1852 Joaquin Murieta was a horse thief.

At the time, he could hardly have been reached for questioning. When the vigilantes were rounding up suspects on November 25, 1852, they could not find him. That same night more than 100 horses were stolen at San Gabriel, and a small posse started in pursuit. Next month, according to a note in Judge Benjamin Hayes' scrapbook, the Tejon Indians again took stolen horses away from a party of Sonorans and returned them to their owner.

"They say," added the judge, "that one of the Sonorians was Joaquin Murrieta."

26

CHAPTER THREE

Debut in San Andreas

IN JANUARY 1853 a bold highwayman and murderer known only as Joaquin appeared in the California gold mines. He could have been Joaquin Murieta, who had bolted out of Los Angeles a few weeks earlier when he was exposed there as a horse thief and possible murderer. Certainly Murieta had been having bad luck at horse stealing, and he needed a new base of operations.

On the other hand, the new Joaquin of the placers was far more savage than the horse thief of Los Angeles. Moreover, there is evidence that he may have been operating in the mines before Murieta could have arrived from the south. For on January 27, 1853, the *San Joaquin Republican* of Stockton gave the first account of Joaquin in the mines, mentioning his name. One source was a Mr. Stevens, who had traveled through southern Calaveras County from Murphy's Camp as an expressman. The other source was an unnamed "French Canadian" who had also just arrived from the mines. It began: "It is well known that during the winter months a band of Mexican marauders have infested Calaveras county . . ." Thus as early as January 27 Joaquin is said to have operated in the mines through "the winter months." How could he also have been the Murieta who had been seen at Tejon Pass in December and at Los Angeles late in November?

As Joaquin is a most common Spanish name, there were many Joaquins in California. More than one of these Joaquins could have turned outlaw on a frontier where the Yankees were still celebrating their victory over Mexico in 1846-47 and were lording it over other nationalities in the newly won prize of California.

Throughout the northern counties they responded to minor Indian provocations by wiping out whole villages. In Mokelumne Hill, one of the richest mining towns in the Southern Mines, Yankees and Chileans clashed in 1849. At a public meeting the miners passed a resolution banning Chileans from the diggings. In the so-called Chilean War that followed, two Yankees were killed in battle and three Chileans lynched.

At the same town *Americanos* tried to jump a rich claim of some Frenchmen; when the latter planted the tricolor on their hill several hundred Yankees stormed them and carried off a fortune in highgrade ore.

Throughout the Mother Lode the Yankees badgered the Chinese. When feuding Celestial companies fought among themselves the *Americanos* were on hand to urge them on like spectators at a circus.

Most of all the antagonism of the Yankees fell upon the Mexicans — mostly Sonorans — who were among the earliest people in the Southern Mines. When Mexicans struck gold on the Calaveras River in 1848, *Americanos* poured in and drove many of them out. In August the Sonorans discovered gold on

28

the Stanislaus and Tuolumne Rivers, founding the settlement that soon became Sonora.

Beginning in 1849 Sonorans had to fight to hold their claims against Yankee jumpers. In June 1850 the Legislature, bowing to pressure from the miners, levied a $30 tax on all foreign miners. When the collectors arrived in Sonora the Mexicans openly defied them.

Not to be denied their weapon against Mexicans, the Yankee miners marched into Sonora. For days the city — and much of Tuolumne County — was in a state of seige.

In July three Indians and a Mexican accused of murder were saved from a lynch mob only by the last-moment arrival of the sheriff. Before their trial, more than 100 other Mexicans were arrested and kept in a corral. On the first day of the trial, when Sonora was crowded to capacity with onlookers, a gun was accidentally discharged in court. From the courtroom to the street, the shooting became general, until the District Attorney successfully pleaded for order. In the end the accused were exonerated, but when further murders were blamed on the Mexican population, several thousand *Americanos* assembled and ordered all foreigners out of Tuolumne County.

By September three-fourths of the Mexican population had left Sonora, plunging the town into hard times. In 1851 the Foreign Miners Tax was repealed, but discrimination against minorities persisted in the mines.

With such provocation, it was little wonder that some Mexicans struck back. In the summer of 1851 the deputy sheriff of Santa Clara County was found murdered and the crime laid to Mexicans. The following November a band of Mexicans terrorized the country north of Marysville, killing several persons and seriously wounding the sheriff of Yuba County.

In his eagerness to attribute every unsolved crime to his protagonist, John Rollin Ridge described how Joaquin himself had committed these murders, but no supporting evidence has ever appeared.

Ridge also, of course, described in detail Joaquin's own sufferings by Yankee persecutors that drove him to a career of bloody revenge. His lynching-rape-whipping episode highlighted every subsequent biography and stands as the keystone of Joaquin's romanticization. For without the traditional motive of revenge for intolerable wrongs, the outlaw hero shrinks to a miserable cutthroat.

Scholars have speculated on the historical source of Ridge's dramatic episode. The horsewhipping scene from Dame Shirley Clappe's *California in 1851* has been cited as the inspiration for Ridge's episode that turned Joaquin into a bitter avenger. This may have contributed to his story and even to some of his actual wording, but the real source is much more obvious. In the San Francisco *Daily Herald* of April 18, 1853, its Monterey correspondent writes of Joaquin visiting a rancher in the Salinas Valley and confiding the grievances suffered in California: "At every turn I took, I lost or was swindled or robbed . . ." More than this, Joaquin said he had lost $40,000 due to American persecution in the placers, and "had been flogged."

Out of this fragment — for there is no other contemporary record of such injustice upon Joaquin — John Rollin Ridge wove a whole cloth of persecution — lynching Joaquin's brother for a fancied theft, ravishing his sweetheart before his eyes, and whipping Joaquin within an inch of his life. He chose Murphy's Camp as the locale of this outrage, apparently because the expressman who brought the first report from the mines came from Murphy's. All the other biographies have rewoven the story and usually embroidered it still further.

But if these are fiction, how much of the San Francisco *Herald* story is true?

First, the Monterey correspondent appears not to have talked with the rancher who had received Joaquin's story, but simply got it at least second hand "from several sources." He therefore could hardly be sure of having Joaquin's words straight as they

These miners are typical of those who sought gold in the Sierra and were plagued by Joaquin. (Wells Fargo History Room)

were spoken. Moreover, the Mexican visitor could easily have been some other character taking the opportunity to impress his host. The anonymous rancher himself could have made up the whole story, and in any case it could have been exaggerated in the retelling. The evidence of Joaquin's grievances is nothing more than hearsay.

We may assume that Joaquin was probably persecuted — as a Sonoran in Yankee California, he could hardly have escaped it. Yet this was to have little relation to the types of crimes — aimed mainly at Chinese — that he would actually commit.

In any case, there is no sure way to connect Joaquin Murieta, the Los Angeles horse thief, with Joaquin, the terror of the placers.

By the third week of January, 1853, Joaquin had left the backwoods of Calaveras County and descended upon the more populous camps around San Andreas. This was a thriving town, founded by Mexicans, whose placers were among the richest on the Mother Lode. Little more than two miles southeast of town was a settlement called Yackee Camp. Perhaps it was so named because it was originally settled by Yaqui Indians from Sonora. But two 1853 accounts call it Yackee's Camp and Yackee's Ranch — indicating that it was named for a local settler.

In any case, Yackee Camp was a polyglot of nationalities and one of the toughest locales in the mines. Around January 20 three Mexicans broke into a tent of Chinese and began ransacking the contents. The Chinese rose to stop them, but the intruders made off with two bags of gold dust valued at $160.

About the same time three Mexicans — possibly the same ones — invaded another tent, put their pistols to the heads of its Chinese occupants, and demanded their gold. When one Chinese tried to block them, one of the Mexicans drew a knife and ran it through him. Then the robbers ran off with two more bags of gold dust.

If this was the work of Joaquin, it was hardly associated with vengeful feelings against *Americanos*. But other crimes were afoot in the same period. Seventy horses were stolen from the hills around San Andreas in one night. The evening of January

21 an *Americano* was murdered at Yackee Camp. Around the same time, another was found dead at Forman's Ranch on the Mokelumne River, and a Chinese was killed at a place called Bay State Ranch, south of San Andreas. These may not all have been committed by Joaquin, but they were attributed to him by the *San Joaquin Republican.*

These outrages quickly attracted the attention of the Yankees around San Andreas, whose suspicion of Mexicans was rekindled. When a Mexican rider on a fine horse stopped at Bay State Ranch, an inhabitant named Hall seized him on suspicion of being a horse thief. After putting the Mexican in the house for safekeeping, Hall stood outside telling the the story to the local ferry operator. At this opportunity the resourceful Mexican slipped off his boots, sneaked outside, and ran up the road.

Close on his heels ran Hall and the ferryman. They were nearing their quarry when three other Mexican riders spurred in front of them with leveled revolvers. The fugitive mounted behind one of them and they raced away, dropping off the road and disappearing in a ravine.

The chagrined Yankees then hurried back to Bay State Ranch, sent a runner to San Andreas for reinforcements, took up their weapons and turned back to the chase. They were soon joined by Captain Charles Ellas, Deputy Sheriff of San Andreas, and two others.

The five then rode after the Mexicans, following them over the grassy slopes for several miles. Starting up the foot of one hill, they spied the Mexicans on top, where they had unsaddled their horses to rest them while watching the advance of the *Americanos.* But the Mexicans had now grown to eleven.

Undaunted, the Yankees started riding up the hill. One of them fired his rifle and a Mexican dropped back out of sight. At this the outlaws on the hill saddled their horses, swung astride and came pounding down the hill. The *Americanos* took cover beside the road and waited with guns cocked.

The Mexicans spurred past, shooting their revolvers. The Yankees fired back, smoke and dust shrouding the mountain road.

Though outnumbered, the *Americanos* had the advantage of cover, while the Mexicans were trying to hit targets from atop galloping horses.

Both sides left the field, the Mexicans taking their wounded with them, the Yankees being out of ammunition.

This battle was described in the *Calaveras Chronicle* and reprinted in the *San Joaquin Republican.* Ridge devoted three-and-a-half pages to this episode, with the two parties playing hide-and-seek among the rocks all over the hillside in a battle of surprise and counter-surprise.

This hill was located somewhere south of San Andreas, and there is actually a 2800-foot mountain four miles below the town marked on topographical maps as Joaquin Peak — possibly from early local tradition concerning this fight.

But in any case, Deputy Sheriff Ellas rode back with his posse to San Andreas. Joaquin and his band, their blood up at the wounding of their comrades, rode another direction into Yackee Camp. There they began shooting at every American they saw, killing one John Carter before they rode off. By nighttime they pulled up at the quartz mill of the Phoenix Mine, where they began shooting at the millhouse. Inside, two Americans awoke and rushing to the windows, returned the fire. They mortally wounded one of the Mexicans before they were both killed by the attackers. Abandoning their dying *compadre,* the outlaws spurred out of sight.

When these outrages were broadcast next morning, the *Americanos* of San Andreas and vicinity fairly howled for vengeance. Three hundred miners gathered in town, organized posses, and patrolled the byroads of Calaveras County. Some of them took up stations at the ferries on the Stanislaus and Calaveras Rivers, which were then in high stage. Others began scouring the hills between, some following the trail of the murderers. At Yackee Camp they routed out "Big Bill," a Mexican who had bragged of killing *gringos.* Charged with participating in the new murders, he was hanged without ceremony.

After clearing Yackee Camp of other Mexicans, just for good measure, the posse thundered southward. At Cherokee Flat the men uncovered two Mexicans, who made the mistake of running. Assuming their guilt, the posse opened fire and brought one down. The other, wounded in the shoulder, was captured and taken to the local hotel, where they strung him to a tree.

The same morning other Yankees followed a trail of blood left by the Mexican who had been wounded the night before by the two doomed defenders at Phoenix Mills. Tracking him down to the river bank, where he had crawled through the night, they found him in a tent and finished him off.

Still Yankee vengeance rode high. Three days after the mass meeting in San Andreas, another was held at Double Springs. The embattled miners passed resolutions approving the stern retaliations already made and calling on all Americans "to exterminate the Mexican race from the county."

"The foreigners should first receive notice to leave," they declared, "and if they refuse they are to be shot down and their property confiscated."

As though waiting for such an excuse to declare war, the *Americanos* were already carrying out these fierce injunctions. A Mexican charged only with "acting in a suspicious manner" was hauled into San Andreas and set upon by the mob. He was almost hanged before the local Justice of the Peace rescued him. By Thursday, January 27, all the Mexicans had fled from San Andreas and the forks of the Calaveras River. Still the Yankee posses searched for stragglers.

"If an American meets a Mexican," reported the *San Joaquin Republican,* "he takes his horse, his arms, and bids him leave."

Such was the result, within a week's time, of Mexican thievery and Yankee "justice." One Chinese, four Americans and three Mexicans were killed, and several more wounded. The races, living together in an uneasy truce, were wrenched apart. No one yet knew the chieftain of the Mexicans by sight. But the *Calaveras Chronicle* assured its readers:

"The leader of the gang is a desperate fellow named Joaquin."

Illustration Page Following: This 1855 sketch shows Moke-lumne Hill as permanent-type structures began to replace tents. (Wells Fargo Bank History Room)

CHAPTER FOUR

Joaquin's Bloody Hour

F OR TWO WEEKS the Mexicans kept cover. Some of them
decamped, and never again would Joaquin command as
many as eleven men.

Local tradition claims Joaquin and his followers hid in two
caves on the side of Carmen Peak, a few miles below San Andreas. But no historic evidence supports this, and they may have
stayed in the company of their countrymen in the few remaining
Mexican camps on the forks of the Stanislaus or the Calaveras.
After all, no one had seen them at close quarters save in a running battle. Not even the leader himself, though somehow identified as "Joaquin," could be recognized.

But on the night of February 7 the people of Angels Camp,

south of San Andreas, were thrown into new excitement. A man supposed to be Joaquin's brother was caught near town. While a crowd gathered the posse bringing him in got a rope and hoisted him up one of the trees on the street. Then they let him down and told him to confess. The half-strangled victim pleaded that he knew nothing of the gang's activities and had never participated in the crimes. Up he went again, so that he might reconsider.

This time, on being brought down, he risked a confession. He had spied on the *Americanos,* he told the crowd, and had reported to the gang the movements of those marked for robbery. At this the enraged Angels pulled him up again and left him dangling.

As though in revenge against the Yankees, the bandits took the road again the same night. But as usual, their first victims were Chinese — two killed at Hawkeye House in lower Calaveras County.

That night the people of Calaveras were in a new fever. A posse of 20 was searching after Joaquin in the lower county. Sentries were stationed at every crossroads and river crossing.

"If he is taken," wrote one editor, "there will be an end to his career."

Just upstream from Lancha Plana a ferry plied the waters of the Mokelumne River at Winter's Bar, which is now under the waters of a reservoir. From nearby Campo Seco, Justice of the Peace Beatty ordered the ferrymen to cross no one at this strategic point.

But at midnight Joaquin and three men rode down to the south bank and with leveled revolvers forced the ferrymen to take them over.

Next morning the determined Justice Beatty crossed the Mokelumne and took up their trail with a strong posse. But as usual the bandits had superior horses and rode through Ione Valley all the way across what would soon be designated as Amador County. At Dry Creek they accosted a group of Chinese and robbed them of $1000.

The next obstacle was the wide-flowing Cosumnes River, flanked by low hills as it passes the present-day bridge on the road south of Latrobe. East of this point, opposite a settlement called Big Bar, the bandits reached the river bank about noon on the 8th. Plunging in, they forded the waters to the soil of El Dorado County. From a store window one Bill McMullen watched them ride into Big Bar, then swing eastward along the north bank of the river.

In about a mile they came to a camp of Chinese at Opossum Bar. At one of the tents they hitched their horses and proceeded to plunder the camp. If a Chinese refused to yield up his money belt, the outlaws roughly stripped it from him.

Unobserved by Joaquin, two Chinese slipped out of camp and ran down to Big Bar. Excitedly, they told the miners that the Mexicans were "no good."

At this Bill McMullen went back with the Chinese to Opossum Bar, where he found the Mexicans had appropriated one of the tents and were taking their ease. Returning to Big Bar, McMullen went up and down the river bank with the news and collected a posse of ten or eleven miners.

As they were approaching Opossum Bar, several Chinese rushed toward them, beckoning them to hurry. One of the Chinese had been shot through the neck, another through the hand. The bandits had decamped up the river with — according to one report — $6000 taken from the Chinese.

Word soon raced through upper Calaveras County that they had killed six Chinese on the Consumnes, but McMullen's first-hand account tells only of the two wounded. At any rate, fired with new determination, McMullen's party rode after them.

On up the river Joaquin's gang next encountered two Yankees; one of them was suspicious enough to draw his revolver. The Mexicans explained that they "intended no harm to Americans" and were "only attempting to frighten Chinamen." The bandits rode on, crossing the river again and stealing three fresh horses.

Moving southeastward toward Dry Creek, they visited two Chinese camps on the way. At one camp they robbed the inhabitants of some $200. About three miles north of Drytown they struck Dry Creek, where they robbed another Chinese camp.

Somewhere south of Drytown the outlaws camped for the night. Next morning they struck the main road (now roughly California Highway 49) and rode on south through Butte City, now marked by a lone two-story rock building north of Jackson. Then they pulled up at Jackson Gate, on the old road just north of Jackson, where they camped. According to a good contemporary source, Joaquin himself dealt monte that night at one of the Mexican saloons.

Bill McMullen's posse, meanwhile, was still in pursuit. The night of the 8th his men camped at Sutherland's Ranch, north of Dry Creek. Next morning, with their number now reduced to seven, they rode on south to Jackson, where three more gave up and returned to the Consumnes. Staying in Jackson that night, McMullen and his remaining four companions — an equal match in numbers to the Joaquin gang — scouted the vicinity through Wednesday, February 9. Back at Jackson again that night, they learned that Joaquin had been in Jackson Gate the night previous. Next morning — the 10th — McMullen and party scoured Jackson Gate. They understood that two bandits were still at the Gate, but no one would point out their location. Exasperated, the posse drove off three horses said to belong to the outlaws, hoping that the owners would expose themselves when they inquired for the animals.

But no bandits appeared. They had, in fact, taken the road again. Near Jackson they tried to stop first one traveler and then another — both of whom got away on swift horses. According to one contemporary report, Joaquin himself rode through San Andreas at a full gallop, shooting three Americans in the neck. The story has no confirmation, and is probably one of the rumors then flying through Calaveras County.

Next day — February 11 — the bandits were still running amok. At Cook's Gulch on Sutter Creek they killed a Chinese. A few miles downstream from Jackson they attacked another and left him mortally wounded. Near the same spot they fell upon an American butcher who was plying his trade along the creek — shooting him three times and stabbing him in the neck. Taking his mule, they pressed northward. Next day they killed three more Chinese between Jackson and Sutter Creek and ran some 50 Celestials from their tents in order to ransack the camp.

Chinese from two different camps came into Jackson with these bloody tales. Every man who could get a horse joined a posse in pursuit. They reached the wounded Chinese and the American butcher as they were dying. Near the place where the three Chinese were killed they caught up with the Mexicans, who were surprised away from their horses. So closely did the posse's shots press them that they took the brush on foot — at least one of them wounded. Somehow they escaped and later stole more horses to continue their foray.

On the same morning, reinforced by nine Jackson men, Bill McMullen of Big Bar took the trail again. The bandits were gone from Jackson Gate and so were their horses. Six of the nine Jackson men dropped out but McMullen pushed on with the others, following the trail of carnage between Jackson and Sutter Creek. On Rancheria Creek they came at last upon their quarry. But the Mexicans saw them coming and rode out of sight.

At this point the other three Jacksonians left McMullen, who rode on with only the three original men who had followed him all the way from the Cosumnes. About noon next day — after the bandits had scourged the Chinese below Sutter Creek — McMullen's party approached Fiddletown, nestled among tree-covered hills along upper Dry Creek.

By this time another of the possemen had taken sick. They were thus reduced to three when, several hundred yards out of town, they discovered two Mexicans lying in the bushes. Unable to identify them, McMullen stationed his two men nearby to cover them while he rode into Fiddletown. But before he reached town one of his men hailed him down with the news that they had discovered some horses in another spot and recognized them as belonging to the outlaws. McMullen then started toward the horses when the third posseman saw another Mexican coming out of town, leading a horse. Abandoning his post in order to notify McMullen, the American left the other two Mexicans unguarded, so that the one coming out of town was able to join them. Two of the three Mexicans quickly mounted double and spurred westward, while the third clung to the animal's tail.

According to local history, a Mexican woman told the Americans in Fiddletown that Joaquin was in their midst. When they discovered him in a gambling hall he leaped on the table, brandished his revolver in the air, announced that he was Joaquin, and challenged anybody to capture him. Then he and his men rushed outside and jumped on their horses while the miners came running after them. One American seized Joaquin's bridle, but the bandit shot him in the face. Then the bandits pounded out of town.

Whether or not this story has any truth — and it is not supported by contemporary sources — the Fiddletowners did in fact come hurtling out of camp in close pursuit, shooting at the bandits. McMullen and his men joined in the onrush. The bandits were shooting back and casting aside their blankets and other encumbrances. Then the one on foot was shot through the cheek. At this, one of those on the horses dismounted and helped him to the animal's back, after which they raced onward as before. But soon another bullet from the miners crippled the horse, and the bandits ran for cover in the brush and trees that covered the hills along the road.

The Fiddletowners plunged after them, but McMullen and his two companions were too exhausted after their five-day pursuit to continue — and this at the very moment when the quarry seemed within their grasp.

Once again — as though by superhuman skill — Joaquin had eluded his pursuers. This was the stuff of which the Joaquin legend was made, though it should be clear that he had the advantage over his pursuers of stealing fresh horses wherever he chose. Curiously, the Fiddletown episode is not mentioned in Ridge's biography, indicating that he was not aware of McMullen's detailed account given in the Sacramento *Union* of February 15.

By this time the people of upper Calaveras County — what would soon be reorganized as Amador County — were aroused to the same fever pitch as their neighbors to the south. On Sunday, February 13, the bodies of the Chinese and the American killed near Dry Creek were brought into Jackson by one of the posses. The outraged miners gathered around the ghastly figures and howled for vengeance. New rumors swept through town. Joaquin and his men had stopped the Sacramento stage and killed the driver and two women passengers. Joaquin's gang had killed a dozen people in Campo Seco.

These were soon proven false, but they stirred the miners to still greater fury. That night the Jackson men held a mass meeting, and nearly the whole population volunteered to join the hunt next morning. A thousand dollars was pledged as a reward "for the head of Joaquin," matching another thousand already offered by the miners of the Cosumnes. A deputation was sent to Mokelumne Hill for more volunteers. Its arrival sparked a second public meeting on the Hill the same night, with the local judge presiding, and volunteers agreed to take the road at daylight. Part of the local militia, the Calaveras Guards, also turned out. Another dispatch was sent to Governor John Bigler at Benicia, asking him to post a reward.

One newspaper correspondent in Mokelumne Hill wrote that "the citizens appear determined to exterminate this banditti." Wrote another, "not less than twenty innocent persons have been murdered in this vicinity within a month," and "robbery is an everyday occurrence." A Jackson correspondent was more graphic:

"The singular success of Joaquin in his daring and numberless robberies, and still more in his numerous hair-breadth escapes, is something unparalleled in history. He is now the terror of the whole country, and no man is safe who travels alone."

At daylight on Monday, February 14, several parties raised dust out of Jackson in several directions. In Mokelumne Hill daybreak was heralded by, in the words of a correspondent, "the ringing of bells and gongs, and the beating of drums, calling men to arms, to go in pursuit of Joaquin and his party."

CHAPTER FIVE

The Pinnacle of Banditry

IN LITTLE more than three weeks after his debut at San Andreas, Joaquin had made himself the terror of the Southern Mines. He and his gang had killed at least 13 people. They had stolen, by one count, more than 100 horses.

Here was, indeed, a new brand of outlawry. Other bandits made a haul and then laid low until the hunt was over. Joaquin kept robbing as he fled — sometimes within sight of his pursuers. He never stopped, even as more pursuers sprang after him as

The Mariposa County Courthouse, (left) erected in 1855, still stood in the 1870s as a reminder of the area's early days. (Photograph by John Crump)

from dragon's teeth. Into these three weeks he had crowded a lifetime of crime.

Yet who knew his face? Those who had seen it closest were now dead. Captain Ellas may have glimpsed it as Joaquin galloped past through the gunsmoke on the hill south of San Andreas. The ferryman who viewed his gun muzzle at Winter's Bar might have caught a dim look — but the hour was midnight. Americans who encountered him in the road by the Cosumnes and on the trace between Jackson and Sutter Creek probably saw his face. Chinese who survived his onslaughts certainly could not forget him — or any of his companions.

So Joaquin now had a face, but who could fasten it to a name? Which of the desperadoes was, in fact, Joaquin? There is no contemporary, first-hand record that one of the bandits ever called himself Joaquin, or answered to that name. From the moment, late in January, that a newspaper correspondent called the leader "Joaquin," the people of Calaveras had used that name. They attached it to every foul deed committed by Mexicans in the county. Considering that the deeds were consecutive, that they bore the same earmarks of brutality, especially against Chinese, and that they were all accompanied by the most daring escapes, they probably were committed by the same gang.

If second-hand accounts may be believed, confederates of Joaquin captured near Angels Camp, San Andreas and Jackson confirmed the name and the deeds. Yet who but his own friends could point to him and say with certainty, "that is *the* Joaquin!"

Nor did any contemporary record state what Mother Lode town he had inhabited at the start of his outlaw career — thus leaving no support beyond Ridge's fanciful biography for an origin in Murphy's Camp.

Still further, no contemporary record before his supposed demise ever mentioned "Three-Fingered Jack" Garcia as one of his companions. Others — Claudio, Reis, Valenzuela — were cited by current newspapers, but "Jack" did not turn up until a Mexican with a mutilated hand was killed at the end by Harry Love and his men. Ridge's morbid details of Three-Fingered

Jack slicing up Chinese were apparently invented to take some of the odium for these savageries off Joaquin, whom Ridge needed for a hero. But far from protesting such butcheries, Joaquin really had no Jack Garcia on whom to shed his own guilt.

In fact, up to mid-February no one had even ventured to give him a last name. He was, simply, Joaquin. His very anonymity gave rise to the wildest speculation on his origins in the press. As usual in such cases, when facts are missing, experts were quick to confide Joaquin's history, and they blossomed forth in the San Francisco, Sacramento, and Stockton newspapers.

Joaquin, it was stated, was about 35 years old. He was 19 years old. He was born in the Mexican state of Jalisco. He was born in Sonora. He had a chain of confederates all the way south to Mexico City. He had a chain of confederates all the way north to Shasta.

In fact, the story that Joaquin was the leader of a guerrilla band throughout California was a favorite. His confederates advised him of victims to rob, and had horses ready for his escapes.

But Joaquin's amazing feats needed no such explanations. Both his crimes and his escapes were impromptu — he seized opportunities as he flew along.

They did agree on a few items that everyone in Calaveras County already knew. He was a good shot. He was a fabulous horseman. His escapes under hails of bullets were near-miraculous.

For the latter the Sacramento, Stockton, and San Francisco newspapers were agreed in providing an explanation: Joaquin wore a coat of armor.

If Joaquin's life were charmed, it was now under severest trial. For two posses left Jackson and two more left Mokelumne Hill the morning of February 14, scouring in different directions. Two days later a fifth party left Murphy's Camp on the

same mission. By the 17th preparations were made in Mo-kelumne Hill to send out still a sixth posse of six picked men under Charles A. Clark, sheriff of Calaveras County and a trusted pioneer of the gold fields.

To these stalwarts every Mexican was suspect. They were, according to one correspondent, "disarming every Mexican they found, and arresting every suspicious person." Early Tuesday morning, February 15, the first mounted troop out of Mok Hill surrounded the Mexican camp of Ophir, some 15 miles below the Hill on the Mokelumne River. Nearby they found a jaded horse believed to have been left behind by the bandits. Inspecting Ophir's inhabitants, they found one Antonio Valencia, whom a Mexican woman had identified as a member of Joaquin's gang. He was brought into Jackson where he was further recognized by several Chinese who had been robbed by Joaquin's band two days earlier.

The Jackson crowd, already whipped into a frenzy by the recent atrocities, gathered menacingly. Valencia was lodged in the Jackson jail for five minutes, after which the mob broke in and seized him. In Main Street a lynch court was improvised, and the prisoner was tried. According to one account he admitted participating in the robberies but insisted he had killed no one. He was found guilty amid a chorus of yells.

Valencia was then taken to a spot in front of the Astor Hotel, where stood an oak tree that had already held four previous lynch victims. With the rope around his neck he was asked to make further confession, but he refused. He was hoisted momentarily in the air and then brought down, but still gave no answer. The local Catholic priest came to give him the last rites, but still he would not speak — not that he could have been very communicative after having been dragged into the air by his neck. He was then, as one chronicler put it, "hung by the neck

Pat Connor (left) was a member of the group that sought to capture Joaquin. He later became a colonel of a California regiment in the Civil War and eventually became a general. (California State Library Collection)

49

till dead." Wrote another, "Not a person witnessed the execution who did not consider that he richly merited his fate."

On two previous instances — once when a companion had been captured at Phoenix Mills and again when a Mexican had been lynched at San Andreas — Joaquin had come out of hiding and struck back. His retaliation was visited equally on Chinese and on Americans, but vengeance is hardly logical.

After the Valencia lynching the band made still another appearance — this time back on the roads near Jackson in the midst of the hard-riding posses. On the 16th the gang stopped a German about two miles out of Jackson on the main road from Sacramento. Knocking him down, they told him to give up his money or be shot. With this kind of choice he relinquished $600. When the robbers let him go he proceeded into Jackson and gave the alarm.

Meanwhile the bandits tried robbing another man on the road between Jackson and Sutter Creek, but his fleet horse carried him out of harm.

Both incidents were close to the junction of the Sacramento and Sutter Creek roads near the present Martell. There was at that spot a large area of uncleared chaparral; it was, in the words of one contemporary writer, "so thick even a dog cannot git through it."

Joaquin and two or three companions were still loitering there in late afternoon when a posse of 20 men, spurred by the German's tale, came thundering up the hill from Jackson. Rifle and pistol balls split the air. For Joaquin it was the third skirmish with *Americanos,* following those on the hill south of San Andreas and the retreat out of Fiddletown.

Left: This is a photo of a purported painting of Joaquin by a young priest at Mission Carmel, near where the bandit stayed while posses sought him. Its authenticity has not been confirmed. (Title Insurance and Trust Co. Collection)

This time he had been inadvertently careless. The posse's guns downed one of his men and — according to the only full account of the incident — hit Joaquin himself in the cheek. Leaving their dead companion, the bandits plunged into the chaparral.

The possemen then sent for reinforcements to help them surround the area. During the evening more Americans arrived, joined by a contingent of local Indians who were induced to help by the offer of $1000 for Joaquin's head. Surrounding the place, they kept vigil through the night.

Next day, Thursday, February 17, messengers were sent in all directions to call forth more reinforcements. By late morning 50 Americans and 100 Indians were ringing the chaparral. Since it was too thick to penetrate safely, the besiegers were loud in their arguments on strategy: Set fire to the chaparral! Cut a road through it! Joaquin, it seemed, had made his last escape.

Yet, miraculously, the bandits got away — possibly even in the evening before enough reinforcements arrived to surround the chaparral. Probably they abandoned their horses — a favorite exigency — and crawled away unobserved to steal fresh mounts from some nearby meadow.

Somehow they made their way south for six miles to Camp Opera on the Mokelumne River, where they stole a boat and rowed across. The night of February 19 they stole some saddles at Campo Seco, thus completing their outfit for new adventures in the familiar hills of southern Calaveras County.

Most of their 11-day foray north of the Mokelumne River in what soon became Amador County was, curiously, unrecorded in Ridge's biography. Possibly this was because he appears to have used San Francisco newspapers in his limited research, and the Amador episode rests on Stockton, Sacramento, and Columbia newspapers. Yet the Amador foray occupies more than half the recorded doings of the real Joaquin. Without it he would be almost what his debunkers claim — a legend, made practically out of whole cloth. In fact, lacking an Amador episode, Ridge had all the more need for the fancy that is the fabric of his book.

While Joaquin's band was crossing the Mokelumne, Undersheriff Charles Clark and his posse were scarcely a day behind. Riding out of Mok Hill on the 18th, the six picked men ranged as far north as Drytown before veering south. On the 20th they reached the Mokelumne River again and picked up Joaquin's trail where the bandits crossed the river at Camp Opera. At this point seven more men from Jackson joined them, and the 13 stalwarts rode on for Winter's Bar to ferry across the river. At Campo Seco they found the outlaws had stolen saddles there only the night before.

The same day Joaquin rode some 15 miles to Rich Gulch, northwest of Mokelumne Hill. On the way he and his men stole several fresh mounts from Americans at the village of Jesus Maria.

Also busy the same day was the Deputy Sheriff of San Andreas, Charles Ellas — the same who had clashed with Joaquin on the hill south of town a month before. Hearing that one of Joaquin's band was hiding at Los Muertos, east of San Andreas, he rode to that Mexican village and found his man, still recovering from four bullet wounds received at the fight with Ellas in January. After a short skirmish Ellas captured him and brought him into San Andreas. There the captive was tried immediately by a lynch mob. When he confessed that he was a member of Joaquin's band he was hanged without ceremony.

That night, as though bent once again on some misguided vengeance, Joaquin descended on a Chinese camp near Rich Bar on the north fork of the Calaveras. Collecting their victims together, he and his men robbed them of an estimated $10,000. According to one report they robbed some 200 Chinese of approximately $30,000 in gold dust, but this report may be rather generously discounted. In the process they killed three and wounded five more. Then they invaded the store at the camp and made off with whatever provisions they needed.

Next day, February 21, Undersheriff Clark and his men rode through Double Springs and San Andreas to Forman's Ranch, near the north fork of the Calaveras. There they learned of the massacre near Rich Bar the previous night. Putting their horses in Forman's stables, they camped for the night and prepared to close with the bandits the next day.

But at one o'clock that night the bandits crept into Forman's and were actually trying to steal the horses from the stables when they were discovered by some Chinese who were on watch. Instantly the alarm was given. The posseman jumped from their blankets and ran for the stables. The Mexicans bolted for their own horses while the possemen fired. One of the outlaws was hit in the hand but rode off with the others. As Clark later reported, "They took to their horses and were out of sight in an instant."

For the next moments all was pandemonium at Forman's while the possemen saddled up and whirled away in pursuit.

The Mexicans scrambled over a mountain and descended on a Chinese camp on the opposite side. There they roused the Celestials and robbed them of $3,000 while the furious possemen were climbing the other side of the hill. As the pursuers reached the top the bandits proceeded to shoot eight of the Chinese — killing three and mortally wounding the rest.

Hearing the shots, the possemen plunged down the hillside and found the Chinese, as Clark reported, "weltering in their blood." The Mexicans had dashed off and were only 10 minutes ahead. On thundered the pursuers, but after a three-mile chase they lost the trail in the dark. Disconsolately they rode back to Forman's Ranch and their blankets.

Next morning, February 23, Charlie Clark and his posse were up before daylight and on the trail again. They came upon one Chinese camp after another that had been pillaged by Joaquin's band. All day they followed the trail of despair, never quite sighting the culprits. About 5:00 in the evening they were nearing Reynold's Ferry on the Calaveras River. As Clark wrote:

> As we arrived on the summit of a hill, we saw them about three quarters of a mile distant, robbing some Chinamen. They turned and saw us advancing, but they stirred not an inch until we were within a half mile of them, when they mounted their horses and rode off at the speed of the wind.

Thus, in the space of 16 fantastic hours, Joaquin reached the high point of his savage career. He had dared to attempt robbing his pursuers' horses, had plundered Chinese camps all day while the law was hot on his trail — first when they were within sound of his shots and at last before their very eyes.

Oddly, John Rollin Ridge devoted less than a page to this miraculous flight of February 22-23. The true Joaquin's career was much shorter than the one created in Ridge's biography, but it contained enough real crimes and hairbreadth escapes to fill a small book, if Ridge had taken the trouble to research it out among the victims and possemen of Calaveras County. American history does not record an outlaw who so flagrantly and successfully made fools of his pursuers.

"We attempted pursuit," wrote the frustrated Clark, "but our horses were worn out and we found it impossible to continue the chase. We went to Reynold's Ferry and remained for the night, and the next day were compelled to return, almost worn out."

Equally discouraged were the citizens of Calaveras County. For a month Joaquin had ravaged them and had eluded every snare. According to the *Calaveras Chronicle,* the spectacle "casts a gloom over this ill-fated country." The terrified Chinese were abandoning their isolated camps and flocking to the safety of San Andreas, Mokelumne Hill and Jackson. Americans with families were considering the lure of the current gold rush to Australia — "fearful, should they remain here," explained the *Calaveras Chronicle,* "of being robbed or murdered." The desertion was particularly obvious along the Calaveras River, which had suffered Joaquin's latest raid. Observed the *Chronicle,*

> It is to be regretted that, so insecure is life now considered to be in this county, in consequence of the recent outrages, that there is a perceptible falling off in the population.

In response to urgent pleas from Calaveras, Governor John Bigler had posted a $1000 reward for Joaquin on Monday, February 21. But after Joaquin's daring escapade of February 22 the *Chronicle* declared that the $1000 was inadequate:

"It has been clearly proved that Joaquin and his party are not to be taken by any ordinary means."

CHAPTER SIX

Descent Upon Mariposa

B Y THIS TIME Joaquin was no longer anonymous. The Governor's reward gave him a last name — Carillo — and a description: "a Mexican by birth, 5 feet 10 inches in height, black hair, black eyes, and of good address."

How the governor got such information is not known. Probably the authorities at Jackson got enough of a description from the many Chinese and the few white men whom he had robbed but spared. The "good address" was also curious — apparently

State Assemblyman Jose M. Covarrubias (left) feared the search for Joaquin Murieta would result in death of innocent Californians mistaken for the bandit. (California State Library)

connoting a degree of refinement unaccustomed in highway butchers.

Another facet to this polished side of Joaquin was provided in Undersheriff Clark's description of the "five well dressed Mexicans, well armed, and mounted on beautiful animals."

Still more ominous, the confederate hanged in San Andreas on the 20th was reported to have described Joaquin and 13 of his men.

It seemed a good time for the bandits to shake the dust of Calaveras from their feet — especially since the whole county was up in arms. South across the Stanislaus, the Tuolumne, and the Merced rode Joaquin and his band on the 24th and 25th of February. Within three days they placed the entire Tuolumne County between themselves and their enemies. By Saturday, February 26, they had stopped among the oak-dotted hills of Mariposa County, where they would rest a few days before try- ing their hand again.

As usual they chose to relax among their own people. This time they repaired to Hornitos, a predominantly Mexican town 16 miles south of Mariposa. Founded by Mexicans expelled by Americans from neighboring Quartzburg, Hornitos was a tough camp that exactly suited Joaquin. Around February 26 he was recognized playing monte in a Hornitos saloon. As the *San Joaquin Republican's* Mariposa County correspondent des- cribed the incident, "he got to drinking and betting very high, and would in all probability have exposed himself to the dealer but for the timely entering of three of his band who carried him off by force."

Less than a week later, according to another Mariposa cor- respondent, Joaquin appeared again in Hornitos on the evening of March 3: "Two Americans who were present recognized him and attempted to take him prisoner, but he shot both of them, wounding one in the arm and the other in the abdomen and succeeded in making his escape unharmed."

About the same time a band of Mexicans invaded the ranch of one Prescot, located near Quartzburg, and ran off all of his stock. Furious, Prescot tracked them to a tent in Hornitos the night of March 4. Then quietly he went about town and recruited a posse of seven or eight Americans, who proceeded to surround the tent. Once again, it looked as though Joaquin and his band had been caught. As the *San Joaquin Republican's* correspondent wrote:

> Prescot, and another young man by the name of Henry Crowell, entered the tent with a light, and seized on one of the supposed robbers, when a party from the outside fired in at the door hitting Prescot in the side and Crowell in the hip.

At this the bandits poured out of the tent while the Americans tried to shoot at them in the dark. A Mr. Levining, with a double-barrel shotgun, was standing near the tent as they came out. He pulled the triggers twice as one of them rushed past, close enough for the powder to have burnt him, but neither barrel fired. Into the night passed the Mexicans — probably Joaquin and his gang.

Frustrated at this double escape two nights in a row (the two reports might have covered the same episode), the Americans marshaled their forces as they had in Calaveras. Several Mexicans in Hornitos were arrested on suspicion of being part of Joaquin's band. Out of Quartzburg, parties of Americans were riding over the hills to find Joaquin. Already a posse from Stockton was in the field.

"It is to be hoped their labors will be crowned with success," wrote a correspondent from Agua Fria, "for citizens are in danger of their lives, going from one house to another." As for Prescot and Crowell, "They will probably recover in a short time to revenge their own injuries."

For a week Joaquin lay low, while Mariposa County raged. Then, according to a story reaching Sonora, Joaquin was seen in a fandango hall near Quartzburg about Thursday, March 10. Someone recognized him and shouted "Joaquin!" The bandit fell upon his betrayer and precipitated a battle between his gang and the local *Americanos*. Two or three citizens were killed and eight wounded before the outlaws escaped.

This story, like the other Joaquin incidents in Mariposa County, has but a single source, and bears the earmarks of one of the rumors that were then sweeping the Southern Mines. Another, showing the fanciful stories then following Joaquin, said that he had returned to Calaveras County and in one evening killed 13 Americans and 28 Chinese.

But the stories of Joaquin in Mariposa County were too thick to dismiss; the quick and accurate shooting, as well as the daring escapes, bore all the signs of Joaquin himself. So did the assault on five Frenchmen camped on Bear Creek, west of Mariposa and north of Hornitos. On March 11 — the night after the reported Quartzburg fight — they were attacked in the dark, robbed and murdered.

"It is supposed," wrote the Stockton *Journal* correspondent, "that the assassins belonged to Joaquin's band, and were, perhaps, headed by the rascal himself."

If so, it was the largest massacre perpetrated by Joaquin outside of the Chinese camps. And typically, he had struck when the odds were all in his favor. The Chinese were usually unarmed and vulnerable. In assaulting Americans, usually armed, he had picked on lone travelers. Once on the Cosumnes two of these had won safe passage past the bandits simply by the precaution of drawing a gun.

Four times — it is reasonably certain — did Joaquin engage in battle with Americans. The first was on the hill south of San Andreas, when he had Deputy Sheriff Ellas greatly outnumbered. The other three fights — the retreat from Fiddletown, the defense in front of the chaparral north of Jackson, and the escape from the tent in Hornitos — had all been forced on him.

But while Joaquin was no *valiente* in facing other men's guns, he was the most resourceful artist in escaping tight spots. By the second week in March he was still on the loose in Mariposa County and the Mariposans were yelping for his scalp. It was their turn to complain that the $1000 reward was too small.

"Will not Governor Bigler," wrote the Agua Fria correspondent, "offer a reward, a sufficient sum to pay a party of men to seek him out, and take him dead or alive?"

CHAPTER SEVEN

"Raise the Rangers!"

OUT OF MARIPOSA COUNTY there now rose a furious cry for Joaquin's head. In fact, Joaquin was only the last straw in a series of depredations by Mexican horse thieves. As the *Sacramento Union* put it:

"Horse stealing has become common in that county, and many talk of expelling the Mexicans from that section altogether."

Quick to seize on this popular outcry was Philemon T. Herbert, Mariposa's representative in the lower house of the state legislature. A hot-tempered Texan, assemblyman Herbert had recently served as a "second" in a duel. He now took the lead in calling for action against the bandits plaguing Mariposa

County. On March 28, two-and-a-half weeks after Joaquin's last exploit in Mariposa, Herbert introduced a joint resolution to provide a reward of "five thousand dollars in favor of any person or persons arresting or capturing the robber Joaquin, dead or alive."

Two days later the resolution was reported favorably, with amendments, by the Assembly's Committee on Military Affairs. The Assembly then sent it back to the committee to bring in a bill appropriating the funds.

Meanwhile, the committee chairman, J. M. Covarrubias, was having second thoughts. Scion of an early California family, Covarrubias was aware that Americans might easily mistake one Mexican for another. In a minority report on April 14, he pointed out that "there are citizens of the State, descendants of ancient and honorable families, who bear the name of Joaquin Carrillo — the name by which the individual is known for whose capture this reward is proposed to be offered. . . . One is a very respectable citizen of the County of Sonoma, and the other is the District Judge of the 2nd Judicial district . . ." (In fact, as the *Alta California's* Los Angeles correspondent wrote, when the judge walked through the street little boys hollered, "There goes Joaquin!")

Covarrubias went still further and insisted that the idea was clearly extra-legal:

"To set a price upon the head of any individual who has not been examined and convicted by due process of law, is to proceed upon an assumption of his guilt. . . . The offer of such reward would be likely to stimulate cupidity to magnify fancied resemblance, and dozens of heads similar in some measure to that of Joaquin might be presented for identification."

Then, in a remarkably prescient observation:

"The magnitude of the reward might tempt unscrupulous and unprincipled men to palm off, by purchased evidence, the head

Governor John Bigler (right) posted a $1000 reward for Joaquin as the bandit's notoriety spread. (California State Library)

JOHN BIGLER
• Governor 1852 - 1856 •
Died November 29th, 1871

of another for that of Joaquin and thus defraud the State Treasury."

For these reasons Covarrubias recommended killing the bill. Though most of his committee were agitating for its passage, the Assembly tabled the bill and later killed it.

But neither Assemblyman Philemon Herbert nor the distraught citizens of Mariposa County were finished. On April 20 a petition was framed in Mariposa and sent throughout the county for signatures.

Citing the outrages of Joaquin "and numerous other murderers and robbers equally courageous and daring," and the fruitless efforts of citizen posses to track them down, the petition asked the Legislature to authorize "some discreet prudent person to organize a company of twenty or twenty-five good horsemen well armed and acquipped" to be called the "California Rangers." These Rangers would "traverse this County and other Counties in the State for the purpose aforesaid . . ."

That no "purpose aforesaid" had really been stated in the petition did not bother the 127 Mariposans who signed it. They wanted an authorized posse to run down Mexican horse thieves without having to observe the niceties of law. The Bill Prescot who had been shot trying to capture Joaquin in Hornitos was still so mad he signed the petition twice.

Soon after another Mariposa County petition was addressed to Governor John Bigler, signed by 100 men including the county sheriff. Approximately a month-and-a-half after Joaquin's last reported crime in the mines, it claimed that "our County is now being ravaged by a band of Robbers under the command of the daring bandit Joaquin or some other equally desperate outlaw . . . Large numbers of Cattle and Horses are daily stolen . . ." The petition then asked the Governor "to call out a company of Rangers of at least Twenty men . . . whose duty it shall be to rid our County and state of the most desperate characters by whom any community has ever been scourged."

Clearly the movement for the Rangers was aimed first of all at aiding Mariposa County, and it was not limiting the action to Joaquin. The California Rangers were to rid Mariposa of horse thieves.

Finally the new petition recommended, "as a person eminently qualified to command such force," one Harry Love.

A swashbuckling Texan, Harry was a veteran of Indian warfare and border conflicts along the Brazos and the Rio Grande, where he had learned the local rule that a good Mexican was a dead Mexican. In the War with Mexico he had been an express rider for General Zachary Taylor. After the war he returned to Texas and pioneered an express route from the Gulf coast to El Paso. Then the call of gold beckoned him to California, where he settled in Mariposa County and became a professional bounty hunter.

Standing six feet two inches, Harry Love was a typical product of the American frontier in the tradition of Mike Fink and Jim Beckwourth — "half man, half alligator." One California newspaper described him as he rode in a parade: "a tall, manly figure, with sparkling eyes, long curling hair falling far down his shoulders, with his knightly sword hanging by his side." But enemies said of him that "he looked more like a large-sized ape than a man, that he was illiterate and a coward." As historian Hubert Howe Bancroft put it:

"Harry Love was a law-abiding desperado. . . . Savages he had butchered until the business afforded him no further pleasure. He thought now he would like to kill Joaquin Murietta. Harry greatly enjoyed slaying human beings, but he did not like so well to be hanged for it; so he asked the legislature . . . if he might go out and kill Joaquin."

Harry Love seemed particularly unlucky in having prisoners escape — requiring that he shoot them, of course. In 1852, spurred by the large reward offered, he and a companion went after two Sonorans accused of crimes in Mariposa County. Near San Buenaventura on the southern coast they captured one and started north with him. While they were dismounted at the bank of the Little Santa Clara River, according to Love's story, the prisoner tried to escape into the bushes. Love tried to knock him down with his pistol, which accidentally went off and instantly

65

killed the man. To the nearest magistrate Love and his friend gave their statement. It is not known whether or not Love, returning to Mariposa without the prisoner, was actually given the reward.

This was the man whom the Mariposans, in their petition to the Governor, recommended "as a person eminently qualified to command such a force from his experience in border warfare and a long residence on the frontiers of Texas and more particularly by reason of his intimate acquaintance with the topography of this county, and his undoubted bravery, indomitable energy, and wise prudence and caution."

With this popular support, Assemblyman Philemon T. Herbert presented a new bill on May 10. This time he omitted mention of a $5000 reward. Instead he offered a bill implementing the Mariposa petition — a company of 20 California Rangers headed by Captain Harry Love. They were to serve for three months at $150 each. Their purpose was to capture the "party or gang of robbers commanded by the five Joaquins, whose names are Joaquin Muriati, Joaquin Ocomorenia, Joaquin Valenzuela, Joaquin Boteller, and Joaquin Carrillo . . ."

Here was Mariposa's answer to Assemblyman Covarrubias. If there was objection to setting a price on a "Joaquin," they would supply some last names — enough to cover almost any Joaquin. The name Carrillo was already established in the governor's reward notice. Murieta was known as a horse thief in Los Angeles. The origin of the rest is obscure, although a much later chronicle makes Valenzuela a robber who operated around San Luis Obispo, and biographer Ridge names him as a member of the main Joaquin gang.

It has been said by later observers that these were all aliases of the real Joaquin. Nothing in the contemporary record supports this. As Joaquin is one of the commonest Spanish names, it is not surprising that it would be borne by more than one California outlaw.

This picture made during the early 1850s showed prospectors in a scene that was typical of the era. (Wells Fargo Bank History Room Collection)

As of May 1853 the only last name attached to the Joaquin who had scourged the California mines was Carrillo, as cited in the governor's reward proclamation and noted in the Covarrubias report. Scoffing at the surfeit of Joaquin names, the *Los Angeles Star* declared:

> It is barely possible that THE Joaquin is included in the above enumeration, but if so his identity is destroyed, and with it all the notoriety he has acquired. A dangerous name is "Joaquin," and all who bear it must needs keep a sharp lookout, especially during the period of service of the twenty mounted rangers. The legal proprietors of some of the respectable names outlawed by the Legislature should petition for a rebaptism.

In any case, Herbert's new bill was referred, not to the Assembly Committee on Military Affairs (chaired by the recalcitrant J. V. Covarrubias), but to a select committee of three headed by none other than Philemon T. Herbert.

When Herbert reported it back on May 11 with a "do pass" recommendation it stirred new objection. As the *Alta California* later observed, "such expeditions can generally be traced to have an origin with a few speculators."

At the first Assembly vote the bill was defeated 21 to 17. Next day Herbert and his friends gathered enough votes to put it over, 30 to 19. Two days later the senate passed it with slight amendments, which were accepted by the Assembly. On May 17 it was signed by Governor John Bigler. To his original $1000 reward was now added an official state posse headed by Harry Love, empowered to track down and bring in Joaquin.

Quickly Harry Love set about gathering his eagle's brood. According to one account he went to the ranch of William J. Howard on Burns Creek, four miles west of Hornitos. A Virginian by birth, Howard had settled in Texas and raised a body of volunteers to fight under General Winfield Scott in the Mexican War. Then with his brother, Thomas J. Howard, he had headed for California in the Gold Rush, settling on his ranch in Mariposa County. He was widely known as a "dead shot" and the owner of the best horses in Mariposa County. According to Howard's later reminiscences, Harry Love was hardly an efficient organizer.

68

"Howard," Love is supposed to have said, "you are more familiar with the fighting men of this part of the country. I wish you would pick the men you consider best suited for this undertaking."

However, Love's own Muster Role of the Rangers states that all 20 men were enlisted on May 28 at Quartzburg, not Howard's Ranch. Curiously, John Rollin Ridge listed Assemblyman Philemon T. Herbert among the Rangers — a most interesting conflict of interest that seems to have escaped the people of frontier California. Actually, he and several others listed by Ridge are not on the official list registered by Captain Harry Love, and now in the State Archives. On the other hand, William J. Howard's claim in his reminiscences that he was a member of the Rangers was doubted for more than a century because he was not on Ridge's list, but the registry of both him and his brother in Love's list in the State Archives fully confirms his claim and greatly upgrades the value of his reminiscences.

Among the others was William T. Henderson, a native Tennessean, a soldier in the Mexican War, and a Forty-Niner. A miner by profession, Billy Henderson was among the shortest of the Rangers at five feet eight inches, but he lacked nothing in energy and nerve. And with Bill Howard, he was one of the two members who left a reminiscence of the California Rangers.

Then there was William Wallace Byrnes, a state-of-Mainer by birth and a Missourian by upbringing. According to his daughter, he was studying to be a Catholic priest in a St. Louis seminary when he decided to run away to frontier Texas. Another source states that he raised a party to kill Apaches in Mexico at the bounty price of $50 a head. But his conscience got the best of him and he recrossed the border, to return later as a soldier in the Mexican War. Taken prisoner, as his daughter declared, he was lodged at a mission in Sonora. According to her story, a young man named Joaquin Murieta was being schooled at the same mission, and the two became "chums." Byrnes escaped and came to California, where he is said to have settled in Hangtown.

Bill Byrnes did claim to be the only Ranger who knew Joaquin personally, but not during the War of 1846 to '48; rather, as he himself declared, "ever since the spring of 1850 . . ." Though Byrnes did not say so, there was an early tradition that he had played monte with Joaquin — some said at Murphy's Camp.

The truth of this claim has never been tested. Contemporary sources do not place Joaquin at any time in Hangtown, where Byrnes settled in California. Nor was Byrnes in Calaveras County in the winter of 1853, when Joaquin appeared as an outlaw and committed his major depredations. At the time Byrnes was in Mariposa County, where he could have seen Joaquin in March 1853, but he does not say so.

In any case, Harry Love's California Rangers sallied forth at the end of May 1853, with only one man — William Wallace Byrnes — claiming to know Joaquin on sight (even this claim was not made until the quest was over).

No sooner had Love ridden out of Howard's Ranch than it became apparent he had arrogated to himself even more power than the Legislature had granted. Far from searching California for "the five Joaquins," the California Rangers were concentrating on any Mexican horse thieves in Mariposa County — as the Mariposans themselves had requested in their petitions.

Using Bill Howard's Ranch as his base, Harry Love claimed by early June that the Rangers had captured one robber and recovered 31 stolen horses. By the 18th they had seized a Mexican cattle thief supposed to be Joaquin's brother, and had headed for Stockton with him. About the same time they captured two thieves and started with them to Quartzburg for trial. The prisoners were later found dead by the road, each riddled with half a dozen bullets — reminiscent of Harry Love's misfortune in accidentally shooting a prisoner near Los Angeles. As Bill Howard later stated, "It took too much trouble to carry prisoners about with us and when we were sure of a man being a bandit we shot him or hung him."

Decaying buildings remain at Hornitos, where Joaquin Murieta once hid, and attract sightseers.

71

CHAPTER EIGHT

Joaquin Heads South

B Y THE TIME the California Rangers were approved on May 17, the mines had been quiet for more than two months. Not since March 11 had a crime been attributed to Joaquin. At the end of March a man from Mokelumne Hill claimed to have seen him back in the Calaveras mountains at Upper Rancheria, recognizing him "by a well known scar on his cheek." But Joaquin had apparently shaken the dust of the mines from his feet at the first furor in Mariposa county. With

Harry Love (left) headed the band of rangers that claimed the reward for killing Joaquin. (California State Library)

73

the whole Sierra foothills alive with posses, his time had run out in the Southern Mines.

Out across the flat expanse of San Joaquin Valley the bandits made their way. Then over the Coast Range they rode, probably through Pacheco Pass.

Late one night in the first week of April, three Mexicans knocked at the door of a ranch house on the Salinas Plains. As the ranch owner later described him, the leader was "a tall, handsome man, about 21 years old, with a long beard, and apparently false moustache, and carried four revolvers and a bowie knife." The other two were also heavily armed, and as for their horses, the ranchero had seen no finer animals.

While hesitating to admit this formidable crew, the rancher was probably a native Californian, and the intruders appealed to him in Spanish. Finally the door opened enough for them to clomp in, Spanish spurs jingling on the floor.

Asking for something to eat, the leader explained that they were on their way south to buy cattle and had lost their way. But though the guests were friendly enough, their heavy armament was enough to make the ranchero and his family respond with great solicitation. Suspecting the worst, the ranchman asked whether they had "just come from the placers," and if they had heard any news of Joaquin and his pursuers. At this, according to the second-hand account of the incident in the *San Francisco Herald,* the Mexican leader changed his tone, placed his hand on his chest, and exclaimed:

"Sir, I am that Joaquin, and no man takes me alive, or comes within one hundred yards of me with these good weapons."

Joaquin — if such he really were — then cooly confided his story to the ranchero.

"I hated the insecurity and revolutions in Mexico, and came here, thinking to end my days in California in peace as a citizen of the United States."

Then, according to the *Herald,* he told the tale of persecution previously related in Chapter 3. At one o'clock in the morning the man who called himself Joaquin paid for the repast and, with his companions, stomped out into the night. Mounting, they whirled off in the darkness.

This tale must remain a puzzle to historians. It was sent to the *Herald* on April 16 by its correspondent in Monterey, some 20 miles from the Salinas Plains.

"I have told this story," he wrote, "as I have heard it from several sources within the last week."

Soon after, the Monterey correspondent of the Stockton *San Joaquin Republican* apparently talked to one or two persons who had visited the same ranchero, and wrote to his paper: "The conversation reported in the *Herald* between the ranchero and Joaquin is confirmed." Yet on the face of it the story is suspect at several points.

Nowhere else is Joaquin described as wearing a long beard. Yet a man on the dodge for many weeks could well grow one, and Joaquin may in any case have wanted to hide the scar on his cheek that had been made in one of the encounters in upper Calaveras County. The false moustache and the four six shooters are too much to be believed, even though Joaquin was certainly a desperate fugitive in fear of his life.

If this was indeed the bandit chief himself and not some other character masquerading in borrowed glory, he said nothing in his vindication about the considerable time Joaquin Murieta had spent around Los Angeles. Possibly he was really another Joaquin bearing the name of Carillo given him in the governor's reward proclamation. Yet the Stockton paper's confirmation states, "The real name of the bandit is Joaquin Muliati" — obviously a corruption of Murieta that would be an easy mistake when the latter name is pronounced in Spanish.

That this night visitor was, indeed, the Joaquin of the placers must be considered more than a possiblity. But his story, undoubtedly slanted by his own psyche and filtered through third parties, must be taken with a grain of salt.

In any case, the "confirmation" printed in the *San Joaquin Republican* of May 4 also declared that Joaquin had been seen in San Luis Obispo "about ten days ago" — which would have been around the third week of April. If the report was true, Joaquin was still in that vicinity by early June. According to a letter from San Luis Obispo to the *San Francisco Herald,* he was "rusticating on one of the ranches, surrounded by a party of some fifteen or eighteen of his confederates, armed to the teeth." When he had been discovered there he even — according to this account — wrote a letter to someone in San Luis Obispo County to forestall any effort to capture him. He would, he stated, "do them no harm, commit no outrage, provided he were let alone," and he would "leave as soon as he was ready for Mexico." The San Luis citizens apparently decided to let sleeping dogs lie.

That Joaquin was heading south was widely believed from Monterey to Los Angeles. On June 11, after some furtive characters were seen at El Monte, the *Los Angeles Star* ventured: "There seems to be an opinion prevailing with men hereabouts, that Joaquin, the robber and murderer, is prowling about in this vicinity." A week later the editor was adding, "That Joaquin passed through this city is just as certain as anything else; and it is equally certain that no one was frightened." Earlier, when it had first been rumored that Joaquin was heading south, the *Star* had cried: "Now let our city or county offer a handsome reward for his arrest, and we doubt not it can be effected, not by Americans, but by Californians, or his own countrymen."

Joaquin Murieta the horse thief was reasonably well known on sight in Los Angeles, where it was generally assumed that he was the same Joaquin who had plundered the mines. Wrote the *Star's* editor on June 18, "Many men of veracity assert positively that Joaquin Murieta and his band are now somewhere between San Juan Capistrano and San Diego, bound down to Lower California."

Apparently the *Star's* observation was somewhat belated. On June 8 a number of horses were stolen from the Californian settlement of Santa Margarita, located on the river of that name in northwest San Diego County. The next evening four Mexicans — said to be Sonorans — drew up at the ranch house of Andre Ibarra, located in the mountains about 20 miles from Mission San Luis Rey. With them they were herding about 40 stolen horses, but they wanted other necessities. To emphasize their demands they drew revolvers and fired at Ibarra and his family, striking one in the leg. Then they tied up the three men on the place, ransacked the hacienda for clothing and money, and raised dust southward in the gathering darkness.

At the California village of San Marcos, west of Escondido Creek, they butchered two bullocks and then disappeared into the mountains, apparently intending to hide out and dry the beef.

Next day, June 10, the news of the attack on Ibarra's ranch reached San Diego. Immediately a strong posse thundered northward out of town and took up the trail of the outlaws. They pressed near enough at one point that the bandits had to leave behind some eight to a dozen jaded horses that could not keep up with the rest. But at nightfall they lost the trail. Through messengers they called upon several Indian tribes to incercept the outlaws. Then they turned back to San Diego with their captured horses — poor trophies from another daring escape. Whether Joaquin had headed this band of marauders is uncertain, but this was widely assumed by Southern Californians.

As the bandits moved on through the San Diego mountains, pillaging as they went, more posses pounded out of San Diego with news of each outrage. Finally, on the night of July 4, the gang descended on a rancho at Buena Vista, below the border in Lower California. There they plundered the premises and rode off with more horses. As the San Francisco *Alta California* correspondent wrote from San Diego, "This is stated to be part of the famous Joaquin band . . ." If so, the attacks on the Ibarra and Buena Vista ranchos showed that, contrary to Joaquin's romantic biographers, he did not shrink from robbing his own compadres.

But now that Joaquin had reached Mexico, did he remain in sanctuary? According to the Los Angeles correspondent of the *Alta California,* Joaquin had been flushed in Santa Barbara County in early July and the sheriff's posse had tracked him to within four miles of Los Angeles by July 10. Reinforced by Angelenos, including a contingent of native Californians, the horsemen rode on to Mission San Gabriel and then to Mission San Juan Capistrano. But their search was fruitless.

A second account in the San Francisco *Herald* also reported Joaquin in early July near Los Angeles, where he stole 50 horses from Andres Pico at ex-Mission San Fernando. Intercepted in the mountains to the north, he gave up most of the horses and rode on to Santa Barbara County. Still another report located him on July 13 in Santa Barbara, where he was said to have knocked down two men in the street and raced out of town, hotly pursued.

Whether these reports referred to the real Joaquin is uncertain. Stories were flying throughout the lower counties, and as the *Alta California* reported: "If all rumors are correct, he was in four counties and two townships on the same day."

By the end of July it was clear that the active bandits had moved across the border to Mexico, which they used as a base for raids into California. On the 30th a San Diegan wrote to the *Alta:*

"It is the general opinion that the banditti known as the Joaquin gang, and other robbing parties, can only be exterminated by carrying the war into the enemy's country, Lower California."

CHAPTER NINE

The Battle at Cantua

WHILE THESE REPORTS were appearing in California newspapers, Love and his men were marching up and down Mariposa County, capturing Mexicans, taking horses and cattle from them, and sometimes shooting them. As for the animals they took from their victims, they gave no account of them. As the *Alta California* later asked, "What did Love do with all

Photograph Pages Following: This view from the cemetery at Hornitos — a town where Joaquin hid from pursuers — shows the typical oak-covered hills in Mariposa County. (Photograph by Victoria Crump)

79

the cattle taken from suspicious-looking strangers?" Not surprisingly, they found no Joaquin.

Beginning July 10, after public reports that Joaquin had completed his escape to Lower California, Love and his men started on a cold trail. Riding nearly 100 miles in less than three days, they crossed San Joaquin Valley and the Coast Range through Pacheco Pass. On July 12 they reached the mission and settlement of San Juan Bautista. In this Mexican community, known simply as San Juan, they quickly uncovered a man whom Love identified as a brother-in-law of Joaquin. As Love wrote to Governor Bigler:

> He says he will take & show us to Joaquin if we will release him. I will try him for a while to see what it will end in. there appears to be quite a number of horse theives hid the mountains back of this place and between here and the Tulary [San Joaquin] Valey. I hope I may make him useful to me in hunting them out.

This curious document in the state archives is not mentioned in the Murieta biographies, nor is the man, surnamed Jesus, whom Love identified as Joaquin's brother-in-law. Supposed relatives of Joaquin's had a way of turning up in the press so often that one might think he was a native Californian rather than a transplanted Sonoran. A brother in San Andreas and a brother-in-law in San Juan — these were claimed in contemporary papers. Later as the legend grew a sister was supposed to have lived in Marysville, another in Mokelumne Hill, as well as a brother in Los Angeles. But these were all fleeting reports and never substantiated. Joaquin's relatives — if there were any in California — were more elusive than Joaquin himself. A sister — which was a prerequisite for a brother-in-law — was never reported in San Juan Bautista.

Nevertheless, Love's Rangers took a man — who may or may not have been Joaquin's brother-in-law — out of San Juan on the evening of July 12. As they left they announced they were heading for Southern California. But after camping on the Salinas Plains that night they doubled back next morning and hid out all day in the hills near San Juan. Next night, still screening their movements, they marched nearly 50 miles up the San Benito River to the Mexican community of San Benito.

For the next few days they scouted the heart of the Coast Range, finally passing through Panoche Pass on July 20. These are the movements later reported by Harry Love. Many years afterward one of his men, William Howard, stated that their hunt had taken them as far south as Los Angeles, and that they had reentered San Joaquin Valley through Tejon Pass. But even their trek across the Coast Range in midsummer, which seems more likely, was strenuous enough.

Love later declared that the men were restless and dissatisfied with the meager expense money of $150 per month, which could not cover their costs. They were hot, tired, and frustrated, and he feared he might not be able to hold them together.

From Panoche Pass they rode south — still in the Coast Range — to a canyon known as Arroyo Cantua. With its steep sides the canyon made an ideal place to conceal stock. Late on the 20th Love's men discovered some 700 to 800 horses under the charge of Mexicans who numbered 70, according to Love's report (86 including their women, according to the later reminiscences of Ranger William Henderson). They were located several miles into the mountains from the mouth of the Arroyo at the edge of San Joaquin Valley.

Next morning, with his force of 20 men, Love rode down into the Mexican camp. Under questioning, the Mexicans claimed they were hunting mustangs — the San Joaquin then being a vast range of wild animals, especially horses. According to Love's report the animals in question were not mustangs. However, when the Rangers took it upon themselves to inspect all these horses, only seven or eight were found to be branded — and these with Spanish brands. Those which Love claimed to recognize he took — the Mexicans making no objection.

If Love identified Joaquin at that time he made no report of it. And if the Mexicans were desperadoes rather than mustang hunters he and his 20 men would have risked their lives in trying to arrest the bandit chief.

83

In any case, Love told them he was heading back to San Juan, and rode with his men some 10 miles back up the canyon. There they camped three days, "for the purpose of observing the movements of the gang," as he later told the Stockton newspaper. But their observation was badly wanting, for the entire Mexican band — horses and all — quietly broke camp and disappeared. When the Rangers rode back on the 24th they found the camp deserted.

Fearing they might lose their quarry, and fearing too that they might be seen before they could act, the Rangers moved three miles further down the canyon before halting for several hours. At two in the morning they were in the saddle again and rode to the mouth of the arroyo, which they reached at dawn. Discouraged at finding no sign of the Mexicans, Love made ready to send part of his company back to the settlements with the little band of horses they had captured.

Then, as the sunlight spread over the San Joaquin Valley stretching before them, the Rangers saw a thin plume of smoke rising on the plain about three miles eastward, along Cantua Creek.

Quickly Love's men rode into the camp, which consisted of six or eight Mexican caballeros and their horses. Whether they were a remnant of the larger band is not recorded. According to Love's later report to the Governor, their horses were jaded, "and appeared to have made some hard marches," so they could hardly have been with the larger party that had just vacated Arroyo Cantua. But at any rate, this new Mexican party was small enough for Love's 20 rangers to handle.

As described in the later reminiscence of Ranger Billy Henderson, the Rangers rode up, captured the two guards and surprised four men who were asleep in the dry creek bed. But the contemporary report in the *San Joaquin Republican,* evidently drawn from either Love or Byrnes, states that the Rangers were 300 to 400 yards from the campfire when they were noticed. "Then there was a hurrying to and fro in the Mexican camp, some running for the horses which were picketed outside — others starting for their pistols near by."

Love raced on into their camp — the Rangers strung out behind him — and halted the Mexicans. They had been sleeping in their clothes — some wearing cloaks and others serapes — and were armed with revolvers. According to Henderson, one of the Mexicans reached his horse and was stopped from getting his guns by Henderson's menacing double-barreled shotgun. A contemporary press report says the man mounted his horse at that time.

While the Rangers gathered around, Love began asking them questions. Most of the queries, reported Henderson, were answered by the Mexican whom he was covering. One current account says he answered the questions through two of his comrades — apparently from Spanish to English. Standing near the leader, according to William Howard, was another Mexican with three fingers on one hand; since he had a revolver in his holster, Love ordered Ranger George Chase to cover him with his rifle and to shoot if necessary.

At this point Bill Byrnes, who claimed to have known Murieta personally, rode up and saw the spokesman.

"This is Joaquin, boys!" he shouted. "We've got him at last."

Love started toward the Mexican leader. At this, led by the three-fingered man, the Mexicans threw off their coats and serapes, flashed their revolvers and scattered, shooting as they ran. According to Howard, the three-fingered man fired two shots at Love — one ball passing through his hair. George Chase then shot back at Love's assailant, the ball whistling over his head.

For a moment a dozen guns were booming. Two of the retreating Mexicans fell dead. According to Howard four rangers —Henderson, John White, Charlie Bloodworth and Tom Howard — shot at the three-fingered man and brought him down with nine bullets in him. Henderson later stated that Bill Byrnes came up and put the last shot through his head. As given in a second-hand account, Love himself later claimed to have killed the three-fingered one in a running fight on horseback.

In any case, when the Rangers rode up and found the man on the ground he had only one round left in his six-shooter.

The hammer was cocked and the thumb of his disfigured hand was on the trigger.

During the general melee two Mexicans were captured and bound, and two others were shot, according to the later story given by Love. Whether their wounds were immediately fatal is not clear, but as Bill Howard grimly put it, "We didn't take any wounded prisoners."

At the first shot the one who had been the spokesman leaped on his horse, bareback, and according to Love's newspaper report, quickly threw his lariat around the animal's nose to guide him. Henderson aimed with his shotgun, but his horse suddenly shied and the charge went wild. To get away the fugitive jumped his horse over the bank of Cantua Creek into the dry bed — a drop of at least 14 feet. In landing he slipped off the horse's back and landed on his back in the sand. According to Henderson, who also leaped with his horse over the bank, the man's hat was knocked off in the fall, revealing the scar on the cheek that was supposed to be the mark of Joaquin.

Next moment the man leaped again to his horse and was pounding down the creek bed. Henderson raced after him. The fugitive flattened himself on the horse's neck. Another contemporary newspaper account says he swung to the other side of the horse, Indian style. Throwing down his empty shotgun, Henderson drew his revolver and shot at the horse, hitting one leg. But on it galloped until its rider turned it up into a gap in the bank to escape Henderson. The latter fired again, hitting the horse in the same leg and apparently cutting an artery.

By this time Ranger John White was following along the bank, shooting his rifle, followed by other rangers. At this moment another shot from Henderson brought down the horse. The man then ran down the wash. After about 30 yards a shot from Henderson hit him in the back. John White's next shot also struck in the back, just above the other. Henderson then hit him with still another shot, which brought him to a halt.

"Don't shoot any more," he pleaded in Spanish, swaying on his feet. "I'm dead."

According to Howard, the victim was raising up a bleeding hand and shouting "Look, look!" when the rest of the pursuing Rangers rode up — "excited, angry, reckless." Without waiting to ask questions they began shooting.

"He sank to the ground, riddled with balls."

CHAPTER TEN

A Study in Fingers

W HEN HARRY LOVE and his band surveyed the battle-
field and examined the hand of one of their fallen oppo-
nents, someone apparently identified him as "Three-Fingered
Jack."

According to the *Alta California* of July 30, "Three Fingered
Jack is an old offender, a consummate villain with whose early
exploits in California we are quite familiar." Born Manuel Gar-

*Left: The town of San Juan Bautista was among the places Joa-
quin hid from his pursuers. Preserving its pioneer heritage, part
of it now is a state historic monument.*

cia, he gained his nickname "from the mutilation of one of his hands, caused by its having been caught under a lariat against the pommel of his saddle, while lassoing a bullock . . ."

It was, in fact, the custom of cowboys, just after roping a cow, to "dally" the reata around the horn or pommel to hold the line fast, and more than one vaquero lost a finger or more in the process.

But according to historians Bancroft and Hittell, Jack had one finger shot off in the Mexican War.

In any case, Jack was described by an acquaintance as having a "disagreeable doggish cast in his features." A native Californian, he was noted first as one of Juan Alvarado's rebels overthrowing the hated California governor, Manuel Micheltorena, in December 1844. With a confederate known as "Mountain Fred," he turned to outlawry on California highways.

In May 1846, following the Bear Flag revolt in which American frontiersmen anticipated the Mexican War and set up a "California Republic," Garcia joined a band of California guerrillas who retaliated against foreign settlers. After the Bear Flaggers seized Sonoma in June, the guerrillas captured two Americans travelling from Sonoma to Bodega, near the coast. Tying them to trees, the guerrillas cut them to pieces. Captured later, Garcia described the incident in grisly detail and became indelibly associated with it in the minds of Americans.

Released on his parole, Garcia broke his word and joined the Californians to fight at the Battle of Salinas Plains, where his fierce action earned for him the plaudits of his comrades as "the bravest of the brave."

Following the Mexican War Jack and his old pal, Mountain Fred, ran mustangs in San Joaquin Valley. With the gold discovery in 1848 Garcia is said to have joined the larger band of Solomon Pico, sharing with him a career of murder and robbery. In 1849 he was jailed in San Francisco, and escaping, had not been heard from until the Battle of Cantua.

Apparently Harry Love or some of his Rangers knew about Jack. They thought him important enough to cut off the head and the mutilated hand of their three-fingered victim. With these trophies, along with the alleged head of Joaquin, the Rangers started for the settlements. But Bill Byrnes' bullet in the head of the three-fingered one had started a spoiling process in the hot California sun that made the prize less than useful evidence. Along the way it was tossed to the coyotes. The hand, however, was exhibited as evidence of the kill.

As early as July 27, two days after the battle, the *San Joaquin Republican's* correspondent at Snelling's Ranch and the *Alta's* correspondent in Quartzburg (both in western Mariposa County) reported that Three-Fingered Jack had been killed along with Joaquin. Shortly after, when Harry Love arrived in Mariposa, the *Republican's* correspondent was writing that "Joaquin was well known in Mariposa County as a notorious horse thief, and as the companion of Three Fingered Jack."

By August 12, when Harry Love was exhibiting the head and hand in Stockton, one Dr. N. B. Hubbell swore before a notary public that he had seen Joaquin in Calaveras County the previous winter in company with three others. Harry Love, who was standing alongside as the good doctor described one of Joaquin's companions, "instantly pronounced the description as accurate" of Three-Fingered Jack.

On this kind of hearsay evidence — all of it obviously generated by Harry Love himself — Three-Fingered Jack was accepted as the lieutenant of Joaquin. His checkered history was dredged up in the California press and his demise trumpeted throughout the state. Joaquin's first biographer, John Rollin Ridge, seized upon this diabolical character as an ideal foil for his romantic Joaquin. With no evidence whatever, he made Jack a leading figure throughout the biography — the blood-thirsty killed of Chinese while Joaquin humored his eccentricity and tried feebly to curb it.

Every biographer drawing upon Ridge naturally preserved and sometimes magnified Three-Fingered Jack. Historians Bancroft and Hittell supported the stories, and Bancroft indulged in some of the typical Ridge extravagances in describing Jack: "How he delighted in seeing them scatter, as with a whoop he . . . dashed in among them! What fun it was to catch them and cut their throats!" In the 1930s, when Hollywood took hold of Walter Noble Burns' *Robin Hood of El Dorado* and made a feature movie of it, actor J. Carroll Naish was superb as the evil Three-Fingered Jack.

Yet there is no evidence whatever that such a character ever rode with Joaquin. He is mentioned in none of the contemporary reports on Joaquin's exploits in Calaveras or Mariposa Counties, or anywhere else in California. The first notice of him is after the Battle of Cantua. Possibly Harry Love believed he could help substantiate the validity of his Joaquin head by linking it with the alleged hand of another known brigand. Though Love was so swift and sure in identifying Three-Fingered Jack, the fact is that neither he nor any of his Rangers had ever seen the real Jack. Since, as the *Alta* states, Jack had been behind bars in San Francisco four years earlier and had not been heard from since, no one arriving in the Gold Rush could have known him.

The only real evidence, since his head was abandoned by the Rangers, was the mutilated hand — as though there could be but one three-fingered hand among the several hundred thousand persons then residing in California.

The truth is that the real bad man, Manuel Garcia, was originally known as "Four-Fingered Jack," according to the Monterey correspondent of the *San Joaquin Republican,* who had known him beginning in early 1848. In fact, the *Republican's* Monterey correspondent is the principal source for the extant information on Manuel "Jack" Garcia. His four-finger count is supported by Bancroft and Hittell, who state that Jack lost one finger in the Mexican War.

But in his haste to identify his victim as the known cutthroat, Four-Fingered Jack, Harry Love was careless about counting fingers. He solved this by the quick expediency of a name change to "Three-Fingered Jack."

It is, of course, possible that Harry was not including the thumb in his count — in which case his "Three-Fingered Jack" could actually have the four fingers attributed to the real desperado.

But in Harry Love's full report to Governor Bigler, dated ten days after the event, he states that Jack died with his thumb on the trigger. If Jack had three fingers beside the thumb, he would not have had to use the thumb for the trigger; only if he had just two real fingers would he have needed to use them both to hold the revolver handle, while using the thumb to pull the trigger. It is not easy to aim any revolver in this manner, but if one holds the gun nearly upside down rather than in the customary upright position it is entirely possible. The point is that there would be no reason for Jack to use his thumb on the trigger if he had three true fingers beside the thumb. In short, if Love's account of the thumb-on-the-trigger is correct, the man could not have been the bona fide "Four-Fingered Jack" of California history.

Thus Harry Love's claim to have killed the notorious brigand Manuel Garcia falls apart. Neither Harry nor any of his men had ever seen Jack, nor did any of them claim so. They produced no identifying evidence beyond a three-fingered hand, counting the thumb. Yet the historical Jack had four fingers.

There really was a Manuel "Four-Fingered Jack" Garcia. But Harry Love's "Three-Fingered Jack" was simply a nameless Mexican horseman who happened to be in the wrong place when the California Rangers came along.

Why did Harry Love palm off a phony hand? Probably he was trying to strengthen the case for a phony head.

A few years later, according to a reminiscence by one who claimed to have been present, Harry Love swaggered into Murphy's Camp to receive the plaudits of the town. In the two-story, stone-walled Sperry Hotel (still standing on the tree-shaded street but renamed the Murphy Hotel) the hero leaned against the bar and told the boys how he had personally killed Three-Fingered Jack.

"We each of us singled out a man," he bellowed. "I singled out 'Three-Fingered Jack' because he was the ugliest in his crowd, and I considered myself the ugliest in our crowd."

That last is one thing Harry said which no one has ever disputed.

93

CHAPTER ELEVEN

Joaquin: Dead or Alive?

W AS THE MEXICAN LEADER really the bandit Joaquin? Harry Love said he was, and later collected a
total of $6,000 in reward money and still more in exhibit fees
from those viewing the decapitated head. Joaquin biographers
from John Rollin Ridge to Walter Noble Burns assumed this
was the end of Joaquin. Beginning with Bancroft and Hittell,
California historians have accepted the story.

*Mokelumne Hill, (left) shown in an early drawing, was a ma-
jor settlement in the gold country where Joaquin and his band
rode. (California State Library)*

But this is not really supported by the evidence. Did Bill Byrnes — even if he had known Joaquin as he claimed — really identify the bandit as he entered the camp? Billy Henderson says that he himself didn't get a good look at the man's face until, in jumping with his horse down the bank, his hat fell off.

When Love and his men examined the man they had killed they found a rather un-Mexican appearance — light complexion, blue eyes, and "light brown hair which is inclined to be curly," according to Love's report to Governor Bigler. Another contemporary description of the head brought back by Love referred to the hair as "beautiful light brown with a golden tint."

This does not square with the only official description available of the bandit Joaquin who ravaged Calaveras County; Governor Bigler's reward proclamation of February 21, 1853, gave Joaquin black hair and black eyes.

Love was well acquainted with Bigler's reward offer, but possibly he had forgotten the description. In any case he was stuck with a corpse that would be difficult to transport across San Joaquin Valley to the settlements. Yet he had to return with some evidence that he had got his man.

So it was decided to cut off the head and bring it back as proof. Bill Byrnes performed this ghastly task, and also cut off the three-fingered man's head and disfigured hand for good measure. Then, with the grisly trophies in a flour sack, Byrnes and Ranger John Sylvester rode across San Joaquin Valley to the nearest settlement, Fort Miller, on the edge of the Sierra Nevada east of the present Fresno. There they hoped to get some spirits to arrest the decomposition of the heads.

But San Joaquin Valley in late July runs well into the 90s in the shade, and at the time the Rangers made their trek there was no shade. By the time they reached the San Joaquin River near Fort Miller the face of the three-fingered one was beginning to deteriorate due to the bullet hole that Byrnes himself had placed therein. According to the diary of the ferryman, they threw away the head and put the other two souvenirs in a whiskey keg given them by the boatman.

At Fort Miller they sought the post surgeon, who provided good California aguardiente (brandy) to preserve the head and hand. Curiously, a traveler at the fort noted in his journal the arrival of "the head of the notorious robber chief, Joaquin Muerto" — obviously a corruption of Murieta — and added that the Rangers had "shot him through the head." In any case, Byrnes and Sylvester waited at Fort Miller for Harry Love and the main body of Rangers to arrive.

At the mouth of Arroyo Cantua, according to Love's report, the Rangers looked over their booty, which consisted of two prisoners, seven horses (all with Spanish brands), five saddles and bridles, five revolvers and two holster pistols (probably single-shot "horse pistols").

Also, according to Love, "the gang had no money in their possession that could be found." Possibly this was due to a "finders keepers" practice that has not been unheard-of in certain posses, but it was certainly odd considering that Joaquin and his band had robbed tens of thousands from Calaveras and Mariposa County citizens.

Nor had the Battle of Cantua produced one single wound among the Rangers — clearly unlike the sure shooting of Joaquin's band in the mines.

If one were inclined to suspicion one might imagine Love and Byrnes counseling together in Arroyo Cantua on July 24, after they had gone among the Mexican group of some 70 mustang runners. If they could just catch some of them away from the rest, they might have reasoned, they could do them in and claim one of them as Joaquin. The Mexicans were probably all horse thieves anyway, and deserved whatever they got.

One may also imagine Love and his men riding peaceably up to a few mustang runners at the mouth of Cantua, holding them in conversation at close range until Byrnes could ride up and shout "That's Joaquin" — at which time the execution could take place in a twinkling without much risk.

Embarrassingly for Love, some got away. He reported to Bigler that "the remainder escaped" after being pursued by the Rangers. These could be available to challenge Love's story.

Sure enough, according to the *Alta's* correspondent in Los Angeles, three survivors of a band of mustang runners — Sonorans and native Californians — returned to Los Angeles early in August and reported that "they were attacked by a party of Americans, and that the balance of their party, four in number, had been killed; that Joaquin Valenzuela, one of them, was killed as he was endeavoring to escape, and that his head was cut off by his captors as a trophy."

The name Joaquin Valenzuela was interesting, since this was one of those listed among "the five Joaquins" in the Act authorizing the Rangers. In fact, before this report the *San Joaquin Republican* was calling Love's victim Joaquin Valencuela: "This Joaquin was well known in Mariposa County as a notorious horse thief, and the companion of three Fingered Jack." But this, as the *Alta* declared, "is *not* the Joaquin after all that Love's Rangers were organized to make such tall walking after. He is not the roving, daring, formidable, murderous, ubiquitous, sharp-shooting and notorious Mr. Joaquin of whose exploits we have heard so much. Is he?"

Added the San Francisco *Herald:* "The Joaquin whose head has been taken off is now said to be that of Joaquin Valenzuela; as there are some half dozen Joaquins there is no certainty that we have the right one until the whole gang is captured."

At worse a horsethief, rather than a highwayman and murderer, Joaquin Valenzuela was certainly not considered to be *the* Joaquin by the Angelenos, who were amused by what their *Alta* correspondent called a "humbug."

At the same time Love also had two prisoners on his hands, both of whom could talk if they could make themselves understood between Spanish and English. According to Bill Howard, "A Ranger stood before one of them with Joaquin's head in one hand and a long knife in the other, from which the blood was still dripping, and said to him: 'Tell all you know or say your prayers.'" The poor prisoner, whom Love later said was Antonio Lopez, refused. The other, Jose Maria Ochova, was said by Love to have identified the head as that of the bandit Joaquin.

Then the Rangers took their two prisoners and their booty and followed Byrnes and Sylvester to Fort Miller. Judging by the record of Love and his Rangers in treating prisoners, Lopez and Ochova were already in danger. While crossing a slough, according to Love's report, Antonio Lopez (the one who would not talk) "drowned himself and his horse." Bill Howard later said that "several Rangers attempted to rescue him."

At any rate, Love's party and their remaining prisoner rode on to Fort Miller, where they picked up Byrnes, Sylvester, the head and the hand. As early as July 27 the news reached Quartzburg, where the Rangers had originally been recruited. On July 31 Love and his party reached Mariposa, where he began giving the press his story about Joaquin, including the claim about Three-Fingered Jack and his hand. Two days later came the first doubts.

> It is remotely intimated [declared the *Alta*] that the reported capture and decapitation of the bandit Joaquin may be a humbug. . . . Perhaps some hombre who had the misfortune to be born a Mexican, has lost his head; but strong doubts have arisen as to the identity of the one now on the way to the capital!

For all his faults Harry Love was a fighter, and he swiftly mustered his defense. On August 4 he wrote his report from Quartzburg to Governor Bigler, describing the capture in detail and claiming, for the first time, that Byrnes had known Joaquin and had recognized him.

"There is not the least doubt," Love wrote, "that the head now in my possession is that of the noted Joaquin Muriatta the Chief and leader of the murderers and Robbers of the Calaveras Mariposa and other parts of the State."

Love then sent Ranger Pat Connor to Stockton with a copy of the report to be given to the *San Joaquin Republican*. Next Love told Sheriff John Boling of Mariposa County that the prisoner, Jose Maria Ochova, had already admitted the head belonged to the bandit Joaquin, and to confirm this a kind of trial was held on August 5.

The only record of this trial is a curious one-page document in the state archives. It gives no name of its author, no place for the trial other than Mariposa County, and no results or findings. Its purpose is to authenticate Love's claim that prisoner Ochova identified Joaquin and his head. It states that Ochova declared the head in Love's possession "to be the head of the great murderer and robber Joaquin Morieta." It purports to be witnessed by "We the undersigned Citizens of the County," but the 18 names beneath (including those of the Sheriff and the District Attorney) are not signatures but are all in the same handwriting.

As a legal document it is worthless; as an historical document it is valuable chiefly for its lack of authentication. On this slender thread hangs the "testimony" of Jose Maria Ochova. He was unable to give any other, since he was apparently lynched. Both Ridge and Ranger Bill Howard claim Ochova was taken to Martinez, near the capital at Benicia, where a mob (said to be Mexicans fearing he would talk) hanged him. But contemporary newspapers make no mention of Ochova's fate.

At any rate, the Ochova "document" was one of the 17 "affidavits" Harry Love later submitted to Governor Bigler in substantiating his claim to the reward money. The rest of the affidavits Love began getting two days later at Quartzburg, where he displayed the head publicly. He had not yet secured a glass jar large enough to hold it and apparently had to pull it out of the brandy keg to show each customer.

With S. H. Keen — local justice of the peace — notarizing the documents, Love got eight affidavits on August 7 and 8. The first two affiants, John Green and Henry C. Long, swore that "the Mexican head now in the possession of Captain Harry Love is the head of a Mexican that was pointed out to me some four months since as being Joaquin Muriata."

Like so many of the affidavits these rest on hearsay evidence — that is, on the word of some other person not present or attesting. Moreover, the man they saw four months before (early April) could hardly have been the bandit Joaquin, since he had left Mariposa County in March.

The next six witnesses all swore that the head was that of Joaquin Muriati, whom they had known for a number of years ranging from two to 18. But none of them stated that Joaquin was the celebrated bandit, nor any lawbreaker at all.

Actually, the bandit Joaquin had been given no last name during his scourge of the mines excepting the name Carillo in the Governor's reward proclamation. The Rangers had been charged with running down five Joaquins, including both Carillo and Murieta. The latter name had not been linked with the Calaveras-Mariposa bandit till he had left the mines and was apparently in Monterey County heading south.

Adding to this discrepancy, two witnesses said they had known Muriati in San Luis Obispo and another swore he had known him on the Merced River — two places where neither Joaquin the bandit nor Joaquin Murieta were ever located in the contemporary public record.

Finally, three of the witnesses — Pedro Montea, Jose Maria Vaga, and Juliet G. Thorp — signed with their "mark," thus revealing that they could not read what they were signing.

Armed with his affidavits and his brandy-soaked trophies, Harry Love rode on for Stockton amid growing doubts of his story. On August 10 the San Francisco *Alta California* reported that Joaquin was even then in the vicinity of Mission San Fernando, near Los Angeles, surrounded with 25 heavily armed men. The *Alta* source was a noted resident of the mission, General Andres Pico, who had led the native opposition to Yankee invasion during the Mexican War.

Undaunted, Harry Love reached Stockton on August 11, where his advance man — probably Patrick Connor — had already struck off some posters advertising the display of Joaquin's head and Three-Fingered Jack's hand at the Stockton House. While crowds lined up to see the head, Love was ready to get more affidavits. On hand to notarize them was A. C. Baine, justice of the peace, who took the testimony of eight men on August 11 and 12.

One of the first was Henry V. McCargar, who swore that he had "drank frequently and rode often with" the robber Joaquin

Muriatta whose head was in Love's possession. Just where he drank and rode with Joaquin he did not say.

Another affidavit combines the testimony of five persons, four of whom said they had known Joaquin Murieta since his boyhood in Mexico, as well as in California. A fifth witness said he had known Murieta three or four years in the mines (Murieta could not have been in the mines all that period, since he was making a living as a horse thief in Los Angeles much of the time.)

Rev. Father Dominic Blaine swore that he had known the robber Joaquin at the Hotel de Minas in Stockton two years before, and that he "verily believes" the head to be that of the robber. Attested by a priest, this is the most substantive of Love's affidavits. But like other affiants, Father Blaine had not known an outlaw two years earlier, since that was before Joaquin's public career; he had to take Love's word that this was the head of a bandit.

In fact, the Love affidavits are more eloquent for what they do not say. None says anything like, "I saw Joaquin commit a crime, and this is the head of Joaquin." None of the witnesses linked their Joaquin with any crime at all.

While Love was in town the *Stockton Journal* said that he had a number of affidavits "from men of respectability in Mariposa and Calaveras Counties, who personally knew Joaquin." The fact is that he had never taken the head to be identified in Calaveras County, where Joaquin had committed nearly all of his outrages. This is all the more remarkable since there was at least $3000 in standing rewards to be collected from various sources in Calaveras. Those who saw Joaquin face to face — the Chinese on the Cosumnes and the Stanislaus, Mexicans at Yackee Camp and Jackson Gate, Americans at San Andreas and Fiddletown — are not among Love's witnesses.

He not only avoided Calaveras County, but in Mariposa County he did not even take his pickled trophy the few miles from Quartzburg over to Hornitos, where Joaquin had also been seen at in least two incidents. Love preferred to avoid these scenes of Joaquin crimes and get his affidavits in towns where Joaquin had never operated.

Only one affidavit might be considered an exception. In Stockton Love got the testimony of Dr. N. B. Hubbell, who the previous winter had been near Vallecito, Calaveras County, when its citizens were pursuing Joaquin. There he had seen a man who met the descriptions he had heard of Joaquin. He now recognized the preserved head as the head of that man.

Such fatuous testimony was really no testimony at all, since it identified the head with a man not identified as Joaquin. Besides, Joaquin was never reported as far south as Vallecito during his forays in the winter of 1853.

This is the body of "evidence" that Love gathered to substantiate his claim. As he sent the head to be exhibited further in San Francisco and took his Rangers on the trail of more horsethieves in Mariposa, it was little wonder that more cries of fraud were raised. On August 23 the *Alta* published the story about mustang runners returning to Los Angeles after Love's party had attacked them.

"It is too well known," declared the *Alta,* "that Joaquin Murieta was not the person killed by Captain Harry Love's party at Panoche Pass. The head recently exhibited in Stockton bears no resemblance to that individual, and this is positively asserted by those who have seen the real Murieta and the spurious head."

In fact, the San Francisco *Herald* had already printed a letter received from "Joaquin Murieta," stating that "I still retain my head, although it is proclaimed through the presses of your city that I was recently captured."

While this may have been written by some wag, a story was widely circulated that Joaquin himself had quietly visited the display room in San Francisco, paying $1.00 to see his own head. Later the San Francisco *Chronicle* spoofed the exhibit, declaring that the head "could only have been displayed by a couple of unscrupulous tricksters the like of which could only have gotten away with this in California." Actually, Joaquin was "believed to be . . . enjoying the cool breeze of Sonora, Mexico without his head, since that is here . . ."

Despite these difficulties, Governor John Bigler was a believer when Love came to him at Benicia with the affidavits on August 27. Forwarding them to the state comptroller, he ordered the $1000 reward to be paid. Two days later Love received his $1000 "for Capturing Joaquin." He split it with his 20 rangers, who each got $42.

But this was not the end of Harry Love's compensation. The following April one of his old supporters, Assemblyman E. C. Springer of El Dorado County, introduced a bill to provide $5000 "for the relief of Capt. Harry Love." The *Alta,* dubious as ever, opposed it:

"Of what Captain Love wishes to be relieved is not stated in the Legislative report, but probably it is of an empty pocket. . . . Has not every man in Love's company as good a title to relief as he? . . . How many men were killed by his rangers, and who were the killed, and under what circumstances?"

Among the four witnesses supporting the bill before the Committee on Military Affairs was Assemblyman P. T. Herbert, who had introduced the original bill to put a price of $5000 on Joaquin's head, and after J. V. Covarrubias had pointed out the danger of encouraging fraud, had then substituted the bill that authorized Love's Rangers. One may fancy Springer or Herbert telling Love at that time, "That's all right, Harry, you go out and find Joaquin first — then we'll get you the $5000."

When the committee reported the bill on May 9 it declared that chasing bandits in the mountains was costly indeed, and that it was "but an act of justice to refund to Captain Love a portion of the money expended by him for the benefit of the citizens of the State." Passed by both houses, it was signed into law by Governor Bigler on May 15, 1854.

Evidently Love had promised to split this money — at least with some, and possibly with all the rest of the Rangers. Ranger Pat Connor made it a point to be in Sacramento on the day Love drew his money.

"I expect I will have some trouble to make him stick to his word," Connor wrote to Bill Howard in Stockton; "may be not, altho I dread it. There will be hell in the camp sure if he don't stick to his word."

Hell or not, there is no record that Harry Love split the $5000. Ranger Billy Henderson later recalled that all he ever got was his $42 share of the first $1000.

The final $5000 was a fantastic prize for a professional bounty hunter to receive at mid-19th Century money values. It was hailed by the Assembly committee as "an act of generosity on the part of the people of this State to one of their noblest citizens . . ." But old J. V. Covarrubias must certainly have recalled the words of his own report a year earlier:

"The magnitude of the reward might tempt unscrupulous and unprincipled men to palm off, by purchased evidence, the head of another for that of Joaquin and thus defraud the State treasury."

Nor was this the end of the reward question. In March 1855 the *Alta* published an anonymous letter claiming that the wrong man had "fallen a victim to Love's thirst for the reward," and that Joaquin had returned from Sonora with 11 armed men to avenge himself. Furious, Harry Love wrote the editors that "Harry Love knew Joaquin Murieta, and *knows he is dead . . .* and that Harry Love never thirsted for the reward offered for Murieta's head, and is ready to answer for his intentions . . ." Even at this date Harry was adding to his story, for this was the first time he claimed to have known Joaquin himself.

For years Harry Love was dogged by doubts and rumors. In October 1856 the Santa Cruz *Sentinel* published a story that Joaquin Murieta "has returned from Mexico," that he had been seen "by a man who knew him," and that his gang was even then stealing horses in Pajaro Valley.

As late as 1879, after Harry had died, the *Alta* published a story about Joaquin living safely in Mexico and encouraging the old story of his death to forestall any efforts against him. The same year the Nevada City *Transcript* ran a story from an "old Marysvillian" that Joaquin's sister had visited the so-called head of Joaquin and had said it was not her brother's. More-over, when living near Santa Clara Love was in a local saloon talking with the boys when someone asked him whether the head was really Joaquin's. "He shrugged his shoulders and made no answer."

But what about Bill Byrnes, the one Ranger who claimed — right after the Battle of Cantua — that he had known Joaquin and had identified him? To more than one person asking him the critical question in later years, Byrnes is said to have replied that he wasn't sure they got the right man. Rollin M. Daggett, a noted Western writer of the 19th Century, knew Byrnes when he lived in Virginia City, Nevada, in the early 1860s. When Daggett wrote a story about Joaquin Murieta in the San Francisco *Call* in 1894, he described how Byrnes would talk about the so-called capture of the bandit. Asked if it was really Murieta's head, he used to answer:

"One pickled head was as good as another if they was a scar on the face and no one knew the difference."

CHAPTER TWELVE

"They That Take the Sword...."

HARRY LOVE WAS QUICK to use his blood money. Two weeks after the state provided him the $5000 he was off for the Eastern states on board the ship *Yankee Blade.*

During the trip the passengers were scandalized by the relationship that developed between two of them, a Mr. C. E.

Illustration, Pages Following: This drawing, from The California Police Gazette serialization of the bandit's life, depicted the rangers shooting Joaquin Murieta. The illustration carried what presumably were his last words: "Don't shoot any more! I'm dead!" (U.C.L.A. Library.)

Bingham and a lady voyager; a committee was formed to deal with the gentleman involved. One of the seven members was Harry Love, who may not have been particularly Victorian in his sensibilities, but who was never backward when a chance for violence offered. In a curious aberration of the California vigilante tradition, the committee took Bingham ashore at the port of Colon, on the Atlantic side of the Isthmus of Panama. According to a report in the *Alta California,* they acted as a firing squad, although only one pistol was loaded and each man was blindfolded. When they pulled their respective triggers Bingham fell dead; Harry Love had no way of knowing whether he could add another notch to his gun.

Returning to California from his Eastern sojourn, Love entered the lumbering business in Santa Cruz County. For years a familiar figure in that county, he liked to appear in public with a long sword hanging from his belt.

In the late 1850s Love married an older woman — a wealthy widow — and settled down on her property in Santa Clara. They proceeded to keep the Santa Clara County courts and newspapers busy with their domestic troubles — as one observer put it: "quarrels, separations, lawsuits, reunions, and a separation again." According to this source, "Harry Love, with all his faults, was the best of the two and the least to blame . . ." But another chronicler said he was "in the habit of beating her brutally, at such times as he could find her alone and unprotected."

In any case, Harry spent most of his time away from home. About 1868 Mrs. Love hired a young immigrant, Christian Elversen, to work and live on the premises — and also to protect her from her husband, who visited her occasionally. Jealous of the young man, Harry threatened his life and ordered him off the place. But Mrs. Love insisted that Elversen stay, and the hired man refused to go.

On May 30, 1868, Mrs. Love and Elversen were in San Jose on business when Harry saw them together. In a rage, he went immediately to his wife's Santa Clara home, swearing that Elversen would return there over his dead body. The old ranger proceeded to arm himself with a double barreled shotgun, a six-shooter and a Bowie knife. With this arsenal he settled down behind a rail fence next to the front gate, calmly eating crackers and drinking coffee.

At home at the time was Mrs. Love's daughter by her first marriage; when her mother and Elversen approached in a carriage, the daughter ran out into the road and warned them back. Misunderstanding, Elversen urged the horses at a faster clip. When they were seventy-five yards from the gate, Love fired the shotgun; one of the shots is reported to have struck Mrs. Love, though without much harm.

At this Elversen jumped down and, revolver in hand, ran toward the gate. Love then fired the other barrel, peppering Elversen's face. But the lad came on, both men firing point blank with their revolvers. One of Love's shots struck Elversen's right arm. Shifting his pistol to his left hand, Elversen leaned over the fence and shot Love in the right arm near the shoulder. With the limb broken, Harry ran for the house.

"Murder!" he cried.

Elversen jumped the fence, snatched up Love's revolver and fired the last remaining shot. As they reached the house Elversen knocked Love down with the pistol. They were grappling on the ground when a carpenter working on the place pulled them apart.

After this the conqueror of Joaquin, romantically called the Black Knight of the Placers, went under the surgeon's knife. His mangled arm was amputated at the shoulder. This was in the early days of anaesthesia, and to alleviate Harry's suffering during the operation he was given a large dose of chloroform. When the doctors were finished Harry Love was dead.

How fared the others who rode out after Joaquin?

One of the first to fall on evil times was Philemon T. Herbert, the Assemblyman who had sponsored the bill to form Harry Love's Rangers and who numbered himself among the first recruits. Elected as one of California' two representatives in Congress, he went to Washington in 1855 and proceeded to disgrace the name of Congressman. While eating breakfast at the famous old Willard's Hotel on May 8, 1856, he fell into a quarrel with his waiter. They began fighting in the dining room, Herbert pulled his pocket pistol, and in the struggle he shot the waiter dead.

Though acquitted according to the liberal interpretations of "self defense" in those days, Herbert was denounced as a murderer by his political enemies at home. When he sailed back to California to campaign for his second term, he was met in San Francisco by a delegation with petitions from voters demanding that he resign. Yet when he reached his rough-and-ready friends in Mariposa they hailed him with fireworks, cannon salutes, and public resolutions in his favor.

However, heeding what appeared to be the majority sentiment against him, Herbert boarded ship and left California for good in November 1856. He practiced law in El Paso until the Civil War, when he won a commission in the Confederate Army. In 1864 he was wounded in the Red River campaign in Louisiana and died three months afterward.

Less heroic was the end of Captain Bill Byrnes, the one ranger supposed to have recognized Joaquin. In the rush to the Comstock Lode he settled on a ranch in Carson Valley, Nevada Territory. When the Paiutes made war in the early 1860s he was seriously wounded, and later was shot again by a woman in a dispute at his mine. He took a job in the Nevada state prison, but the 31 wounds — three near his heart and one in his head — that he had suffered in his long career as a frontier adventurer finally caught up with him. In an effort to relieve his discomfort, San Francisco doctors removed nine bullets from his body. But at 50 his mind began to fail. According to his daughter, "his wounds were very painful at times, and at last they drove him insane." In 1873 he was sent to the Stockton asylum, where he died the next year.

So it went with the others. John White, one of the two rangers who had shot the man they called Joaquin, was killed soon afterward near Fort Tejon — by Mexican avengers, according to one account. Another was killed at Santa Cruz — allegedly in the same manner — and still another was assassinated by a Mexican in Contra Costa County. Two were killed in a gunfight at Salt Lake. Another joined the gold rush to British Columbia and was drowned in the Fraser River. Still another joined William Walker's filibustering expedition to Nicaragua and was killed in that country. And another joined Herbert among the casualties in the Civil War. Not all, but a remarkable proportion of, the Rangers had fulfilled the Biblical prophecy, "They that take the sword shall perish by the sword."

Only one ranger went on to become more famous in his subsequent career. Patrick Edward Connor, who had served gallantly as an officer in the Mexican War, was commissioned a colonel of a California regiment in the Civil War. He won a general's rank fighting Indians in the Rockies and was still in service when he died in 1891.

Among the last of the rangers was William J. Howard, who was supposed to have provided the recruiting place for Love's band at his ranch on Burns Creek in Mariposa County. Beginning in 1889 he gave several newspaper interviews about the capture and death of Joaquin and the later fate of the various rangers. Since he was not listed as a ranger in John Rollin Ridge's biography, his reminiscences were suspect for many years. But in 1967 publisher William Secrest of Fresno discovered in the State Archives a muster roll of the California Rangers, dated only three days after the battle at Cantua Creek and in Harry Love's own hand. It contained Howard's name, as well as that of his brother, thus greatly enhancing the credibility of his narratives.

The only other ranger to leave a reminiscence was William T. Henderson, who was interviewed by the *Fresno Expositor* in November 1879 (the story was reprinted in at least two other California newspapers). In this chronicle Henderson confirmed that he and White had been the ones who killed the Mexican leader they called Joaquin.

A few years after the Murieta affair, the old Tennessee soldier went over the Sierra Nevada to the mines of the Inyo region. There he was the first to climb Telescope Peak, the 11,000-foot mountain that is the highest bordering Death Valley. In 1863 Henderson was part of a posse that pursued and killed nine

113

Paiutes and later the same year killed others in a running battle in Panamint Valley. After participating in a number of mining ventures he returned to San Joaquin Valley and settled near Fresno.

For years before he died at Coarse Gold in 1882, according to one account, Henderson was bothered by dreams in which the decapitated Joaquin would accost him and ask for his head.

Finally, what about the head itself? After being exhibited in San Francisco by members of the rangers, it was sold to others, and passed from hand to hand until it rested in the Academy of Science in San Francisco. Some time in the late 1890s it was lost from public record, though a tradition developed that it was destroyed in the 1906 fire. The men who brought in the head, and even the head itself, were gone at last.

It was, in fact, curious that only two of the rangers publicly talked about the killing of Joaquin, and they waited more than two decades after the event. Not the rangers, but non-witness writers, had long since ballooned the Joaquin story into what Franklin Walker has called "the most interesting of Western legends."

Chapter Thirteen

The Myth-Makers

L ESS THAN A YEAR after Joaquin's lightning career —
that is, about the time Harry Love got his $5000 reward
from the state legislature — the Joaquin biographers moved in.

In May 1854 appeared "Joaquin the Mountain Robber, or
the Bandits of the Sierra Nevada," in the first and only issue
of the *Pacific Police Gazette*. No copy of this "biography" has
ever come to light.

Two months later — on July 9, 1854 — the first issue of a
California Police Gazette offered chapters I and II of "Joaquin,
the Mountain Robber! Or the Guerilla of California." Only the
second issue of this weekly paper, containing chapters III and
IV, has survived through one copy now in the Princeton Uni-

versity Library. In it neither Murieta nor any other last name is given, but in a curious throwback to the period of the bandit's actual exploits in Calaveras County, he is simply called "Joaquin."

This is just about the only similarity with the facts in this earliest fragment of a "biography." Written in the florid style of the penny dreadfuls, it introduces Harry Love as Joaquin's foe early in the story. The only contemporary reference that it uses is the unconfirmed newspaper item that Joaquin "rode through the village of San Andreas at a quick gallop, and without cause shot three Americans as he passed through the streets." Its value as history can be gauged by the following quote from Joaquin as he dashes into the cave where his comrades are hiding:

> Our foes! the American miners who haunt us through the mountains like starving wolves in pursuit of prey, are now in the glen! There is no time to loose! Let's away through yonder side retreat, rush on the dastard knaves, my brave comrades, and suffer not one of them to escape to tell of their defeat. Thus will Joaquin avenge himself on these bold Americans who dare to hunt him from his lair.

Within a month of the *California Police Gazette* "Life," a third biography of Joaquin was published by W. B. Cooke of San Francisco. A 90-page narrative without chapter divisions, it was titled *Life and Adventures of Joaquin Murieta, the Celebrated California Bandit*. Its author was shown simply as "Yellow Bird," but this was the Indian name of John Rollin Ridge, a half-Cherokee who had come to California from the Indian Territory in 1850. Tall and attractive, he had an intense, sensitive countenance wreathed in luxuriant black hair and beard. He looked somewhat wild and unpredictable, but in fact he was thoroughly civilized in the tradition of his advanced tribe.

Ridge had ample reason to be attracted by a subject such as a Mexican bandit in American California. He was the son and grandson of chiefs who had signed the agreement calling for the "Trail of Tears" relocation of the Cherokees from Georgia to Indian Territory in 1836. He had seen his father assassinated

by members of a rival Cherokee faction. He had vowed revenge against each of the assassins, and he had killed one of his enemies — possibly in self-defense. Fleeing Indian Territory, he tried unsuccessfully to raise money for a trial.

An outlaw among his own people, Ridge joined the Gold Rush to California. There he met failure again in mining for gold, and still again in the trading business. At the time of Joaquin's public career, or shortly thereafter, Ridge was a Deputy Clerk, Auditor, and Recorder of Yuba County, in the Northern Mines.

By early 1854 he was writing poems and stories for the *Pioneer,* a San Francisco magazine, and still later contributed to the *Golden Era* and the *Hesperian.* The Joaquin saga seized his imagination, and he plunged into the story with visions of an author's fortune dancing in his mind.

It has been claimed by literary scholars that Ridge created Joaquin "practically out of whole cloth." This is not really the case. It is clear that he used some, though probably not many, of the Joaquin reports in contemporary newspapers. Whether he visited any of the scenes of Joaquin's actual exploits may only be conjectured, and while he could have written the whole story from newspaper files and his own imagination, he does show thorough familiarity with the Calaveras County geography of that day.

He is especially detailed in his description of events and his identification of possemen in the episodes south of San Andreas in late January 1853 (these are the opening events in the public record of Joaquin's bandit career, but appear two-thirds of the way into the Ridge account). His misspelling of some place names elsewhere, such as Arroyo Cantoova (Cantua) and Oenitas (Hornitos) differs from equally bad misspellings in the newspapers, and suggests that he might have used some oral interviews, possibly of Harry Love or of Deputy Sheriff Charles A. Ellas of Calaveras County.

In any case, the last third of Ridge's narrative is simply an embroidered version of the episodes chronicled in the public press from January to August, 1853. This section differs markedly from the first two-thirds in being largely expository, with little conversation by Joaquin and his gang. True, Ridge injects Three-fingered Jack where none appeared in the press accounts, but neither Rosita nor any other paramour figures in these latter pages.

Curiously, Ridge leaves out Joaquin's entire foray into the edge of El Dorado County and what soon became Amador County — the trail of robberies along the Cosumnes River, the comical flight out of Fiddletown, the murders around Jackson and the escape from the chaparral thicket north of that town. Except for these omissions and some conversational embellishments, the last one-third of Ridge's book (starting on page 109 of the 1955 republished edition) is not too far from the facts.

Far different is the first two-thirds, which is almost pure invention. The lynching of Joaquin's brother, the rape of Rosita, Joaquin's vengeful pursuit and murder of those responsible, the bloody antics of Three-fingered Jack — all are the creation of Ridge's imagination.

It is possible, however, to identify certain newspaper items that obviously stirred his fancy. The horsewhipping episode he developed from a suggestion in a Joaquin "interview" on the Salinas Plain in the *San Francisco Herald* of April 18, 1853. From the *Alta California* of November 15, 1852, he got the idea for the episode in which Joaquin and Three-fingered Jack assassinate General Joshua H. Bean. Out of a few newspaper accounts of unsolved crimes committed in 1851 and '52, Ridge laid a frightful catalogue of evil at Joaquin's door.

Yet he also idealized his hero with the gallant attributes of mercy to the unfortunate, sentimental camaraderie with his friends, kindness to his sweetheart, and visionary planning for

119

revolution against his American oppressors. A worthy analysis of Ridge's deepseated motivations in creating such a Joaquin has been given by Franklin Walker in his *San Francisco's Literary Frontier:*

> ... in supporting the Mexican cause, the cause of the down-and-outer, he was supporting the minority cause of his fellow Indians, whom he had seen mistreated and driven from their lands when he was a boy. In telling of Joaquin's plans to strike a blow for his people, he was expressing his own lifelong hopes to help the Cherokees regain their place in the sun. And, finally, in having Joaquin achieve his revenge by wiping out his degraders one by one, Ridge was vicariously blotting out each of the assassins who had driven their knives into the body of his father.

Yet Ridge was also human enough to know what humans wanted in a story. He wrote in an age of the penny dreadful and the dime novel, and other such writings before and after his own seized upon the Joaquin saga as a natural. Ridge's is a book of undressed passions. Joaquin and his companions act and react with unbridled emotion. They do things that Ridge's "civilized" readers could never do, and for this very reason they have a basic human appeal.

And in a way, although Ridge's hero committed innumerable black crimes, his story carried with it a certain moral that needed telling in 19th Century California. Joaquin left behind the lesson that, as Ridge put it, "there is nothing so dangerous in its consequences as *injustice* to *individuals* — whether it arise from prejudice of color or from any other source; that a wrong done to one man is a wrong to society and to the world."

Many Californians undoubtedly knew when they read Ridge's little book that it was mostly fancy. In the only notice of the book in the San Francisco press, the *California Chronicle* observed that it "may serve as very amusing reading for Joaquin Murieta, should he get hold of it . . ." The picture of Harry Love "does not look at all like him," and as for the imaginative tale itself, "If the lives of all the Joaquins that ever cut a purse could be written, they would not contain the horrid catalogue in this book."

Ridge's venture as an author was scarcely more rewarding than his other efforts in California. Two months after his book appeared, he was writing to his cousin that his publishers had absconded without paying him after selling 7,000 copies (not bad for a California book at that time). But he went on with his career as a journalist and poet — first on the young *Sacramento Bee,* then to become editor of the newspaper at Oroville, to which he took a young bride in 1857. At that time the *Alta California* put in a generous word: "His writings have been distinguished by dignity, ability and good sense. . . . has shown a capacity . . . to touch the citadel of the soul."

Ridge next became editor of the *Marysville Express,* then the *Marysville National Democrat,* the *San Francisco Herald,* and the *Grass Valley National.* Known as a vigorous Douglas Democrat, Ridge had been a slaveholder in Indian Territory, and one of his detractors in California claimed that he "believed negro bondage to be a divine institution; was against the war on the part of freedom, and for anything Southern . . ."

About 1865 Ridge journeyed eastward to rally his father's faction in the Cherokee tribe and assert his claim as chieftain. But he returned in disappointment to his editor's desk in Grass Valley, where he fell into a state of mental depression. He died of "brain fever" on October 5, 1867, leaving his wife and a child. Again the *Alta* was ready with a laudatory obituary, but it was a curious commentary on his Joaquin story — Ridge's only book — that it was not even mentioned in the lengthy obituaries in such newspapers as the *Alta* and the *Sacramento Bee.*

But a few years later a new publisher came forth with another version, claiming that before his death Ridge had "prepared a revised edition of his story of Joaquin Murieta, to which he had added much new and heretofore unpublished material." This 1871 edition included a short preface purporting to have been written by Ridge before he died in 1867. Yet one may feel just a little uneasy about Ridge's participation in this edition. It does contain some new material — such as more vivid embellishment of the early raping-hanging-whipping episodes and a new Joaquin foray over the Sierra Nevada to Mono Lake. Obviously

121

the new publishers needed "much new and heretofore unpublished material" in order to promote sales, and it is somewhat too convenient that Ridge himself had provided just that, complete with preface, four years before.

In any case, the 1871 edition was more widely received than the 1854 version and more influential in spreading the Joaquin legend. In 1888 Hubert Howe Bancroft, the patriarch among California historians, used this edition as the principal source of his narrative on Joaquin in the book, *California Pastoral.* Bancroft's 20 pages on Joaquin is practically a digest of Ridge's book, although it is possible to identify at least one newspaper source — the *San Francisco Herald's* April 18, 1853 "interview" on the Salinas Plains.

Then in 1897 Theodore Hittell, California's other leading historian of the 19th Century, devoted a 15-page chapter to "Joaquin Murieta and his Banditti," doing better than Bancroft in footnoting Ridge's 1871 edition on seven of the pages.

In thus swallowing the Ridge story without question, Bancroft and Hittell violated their own research standards and put the imprimatur on the Joaquin legend down to the present day. Perhaps they accepted Ridge as being obviously more respectable then the spate of lurid Murieta "biographies" and romances which by the 1890s had saturated the paperback market.

The first of these was "The Life of Joaquin Murieta, Brigand Chief of California," printed in 10 weekly installments in a new *California Police Gazette* from September 3 to November 5, 1859. Three weeks after the last issue it was printed in a 71-page pamphlet. Illustrated by the noted California artist, Charles C. Nahl, the anonymous *Police Gazette* version was even more dramatically written than Ridge's. Except for giving

Mrs. John Rollin Ridge (left) became the author's wife in 1857. After his book, he continued his career as editor of newspapers in gold country communities. (California State Library)

123

Joaquin two mistresses — Carmela and Clarita — it followed the Ridge story so closely that it was obvious piracy. Nor could the *Police Gazette* stand on the claim that history is anybody's domain, since Ridge himself had invented most of the episodes used by the *Gazette*. He was powerfully aware of this when he cried "plagiarism!" in the *Marysville Express*. If he did participate in his later 1871 edition, sardonically labelled the Third Edition in apparent reference to the *Police Gazette* pirating, he returned the compliment by adopting and expanding a Mono Lake episode that had first appeared in the *Police Gazette* version.

Despite Ridge's protests, it was the *Police Gazette* story that became the basis of most subsequent Joaquin books. As early as 1865 a New York publisher turned out a *Joaquin (the Claude Duval of California); or the Marauder of the Mines* — Duval being an English highwayman of the 17th Century. Beadle's Dime Library of New York followed in 1881 with two short volumes on Joaquin by one Joseph E. Badger, Jr. Then the tale jumped to France, where a book by Robert Hyenne is known only through a Spanish translation published in Santiago, Chile, in 1906. In it, as might be expected, Joaquin becomes *El Bandido Chileno*. A further edition of this one in Barcelona and Mexico City opened two other countries to the Joaquin legend, with a subsequent 206-page biography by "El Professor Acigar," published in Barcelona and another (naturally restoring Joaquin to his proper Sonoran heritage) in Mexico City by Ireneo Paz (1908).

As the tale traveled further in time and space from mid-19th Century California it took on still more accretions of fancy. The great-great grandfather of these later volumes — the *California Police Gazette* edition of 1859 — was only 71 pages. But Acigar's Barcelona version was 206 pages and the Mexico City publication of Ireneo Paz was 281 pages — the differences being manufactured out of the rich Latin imagination. By the time the Spanish tale was translated back into English in a Chicago 1925 edition, its *Police Gazette* parentage was still provable, but Joaquin's mistress had become his wife and was renamed

Carmen. To complete the circle, a mountain south of San Andreas containing a "Joaquin cave" was appropriately named Carmen Peak.

By this time Joaquin Murieta (or Murietta, or Murrieta, as his name was spelled in later versions) had become an international hero. Whenever a writer needed a sure-fire formula he seemed to turn naturally in the direction of Joaquin. Possibly the high point of Joaquin fever was reached with the "Loves of Lola Montez," a serialized tale in the *San Francisco Call* by Evelyn Wells, in which Joaquin becomes a lover of that celebrated California femme fatale.

To trace the flood of later "biographies" and romances in two languages about the famed California bandit would only be an exercise in bibliographic virtuosity; like their predecessors they had nothing to do with the real Joaquin and were simply capitalizing on the fame achieved for him by the earliest tales. Numbering at least a dozen (so far as is known), the Joaquin stories are cited in the bibliography of this book.

In the 20th Century local historians such as James C. Cunningham conscientiously picked up fragments of Murietana from people claiming to have known the bandit at least 70 years earlier. Besides suffering the erosion of memory and the accretions of telling and retelling, such tales are subject to the familiar human propensity for attaching one's self to legendary characters. Some of them depend on the story-teller's being more than 100 years old. They may be true, and again they may not.

In 1932 appeared a thorough retelling of the Joaquin story in *The Robin Hood of El Dorado,* by Walter Noble Burns. Well-known to Western fans as the author of *Tombstone* and *The Saga of Billy the Kid,* Burns was a better writer than an historian. He accepted uncritically the earliest tales, reconciling the differences in the name of Joaquin's sweetheart by calling her Rosita Carmel. He also added another gyration to the Joaquin yarn by throwing together the episodes at random — out of any chronological order.

Literary critic Joseph Henry Jackson was too harsh on Burns

in saying that *The Robin Hood of El Dorado* was simply "a gathering and rewriting of whatever else had been printed about Murieta, beginning with Ridge . . ." While Burns did rely on the "biographies" for the bulk of his story, he obviously did some research at the California State Library at Sacramento, where newspaper references on any subject are well catalogued. But this mainly served to strengthen the latter part of his book — the expedition of Harry Love's Rangers and the subsequent myths of Joaquin's escapes and reappearances. Burns missed, as did all the others, the Gold Country newspaper accounts detailing the real Joaquin's exploits in the winter of 1853.

Meanwhile, the Joaquin saga was being sung by still more dramatic bards — the poet and the playwright. Cincinnatus Hiner Miller, a noted California writer who had transferred to Oregon, wrote a 30-page poem on *Joaquin*. Published at the head of Miller's collected poems in both England and Oregon, it had nothing to do with the real Joaquin and little to do with the Ridge Joaquin (the bandit is simply riding furiously through the Sierra, wounded by pursuers, to die in the arms of a sympathetic priest). But Miller went even farther than the others in purifying Joaquin as a kind of California Galahad. As Joaquin breathes his last, Miller writes: "Here lies a youth whose fair face is Still holy from a mother's kiss."

A result which far outlasted the poem itself was the fact that Miller adopted "Joaquin" as his first name; with his new penname, half-borrowed from a vicious murderer, Joaquin Miller won his place among famed Western writers.

As early as 1858 Joaquin went on the San Francisco stage in a five-act play by Charles E. B. Howe, who made the bandit a pure Castilian and named his sweetheart "Belloro." In 1927 the scion of an early California family, B. Ignacio Ortega, wrote a pageant on the life of "that most romantic of all early Californians, Joaquin Murietta, the love bandit." Five years later a romantic comedy on the life of Murieta was written by Dr. Charles D. McGettigan and presented with a "cast of 35" on the San Francisco stage. In Santiago, Chile, a *Joaquin Murieta* in six acts was written by A. Acevedo Hernandez in 1936. As

126

late as 1967 one Pablo Neruda of Santiago wrote still another play on Murieta.

But the ultimate dramatization was a Class A Hollywood motion picture, *The Robin Hood of El Dorado,* produced in 1936 with Warner Baxter in the title role. Filling the screen with gunpowder and thunderous hoofbeats, it completed the projection of Joaquin into the epic mold.

Accompanying the movie was a serialization in newspapers across the country by the noted western writer Peter B. Kyne. Also entitled *The Robin Hood of El Dorado,* it was acknowledged as an adaptation of the "novel" by Walter Burns in advertisements which also claimed that "every word of his amazing story is true."

By now the original Cherokee journalist with a heart for the oppressed had scored far greater than he dreamed. His philosophy of justice and injustice had reached not just 7,000, but the millions. As for Joaquin, he had grown from a fleeting Calaveras County cutthroat to a fabulous knight errant immortalized on three continents. As Ridge himself wrote: "so trivial are the circumstances which often determine the fortunes of men!"

127

Act of Congress in the year 1857, by Kuchel & Dresel in the Clerks Office of the

JACKSON,

AMADOR COUNTY, CAL.

1857.

CHAPTER FOURTEEN

"Joaquin Slept Here"

WHEN THIS WRITER first toured the Mother Lode in 1939 he visited Murphy's Camp, by then a charming remnant of a Gold Rush town. In the barroom of the old two-story Murphy Hotel, a local sage pointed solemnly to the door casing at the front entrance.

"See them bullet holes? That's where Joaquin Murieta shot it out with the sheriff."

Dutifully, I examined the holes with appropriate awe, in-

Jackson (left) was among the larger towns in the gold country where Joaquin's band preyed on miners. (California State Library Collection)

wardly recalling that the hotel was built two years after the end of Joaquin's career.

Up and down the Mother Lode, the Gold Rush towns appropriated Joaquin Murieta. He slept here, he "used to play cards" there, he hid out over yonder. From a fleeting figure who almost never showed himself, Joaquin was transformed into the most gregarious, spotlight-loving fellow on the Lode. Almost every town produced its "oldest inhabitant" who was a personal friend of Murieta. For an outlaw constantly on the dodge, Joaquin cultivated more friends than any politician in California.

The "I knew Joaquin" game began, naturally enough, with the hunt for his "buried treasure." Contemporary newspaper accounts of his exploits showed a total of approximately $21,-000 in gold and some 120 horses actually stolen by his gang. But Californians insisted on believing that a fabulous treasure had been buried and never recovered. Pick-and-shovel expeditions were set in motion by each new rumor that a mysterious Mexican had appeared in the settlements with a tattered map, muttering words about "Joaquin's treasure."

In April 1883 the *Fresno Expositor* described how the gang had hidden more than $100,000 "at some secluded spots in the Coast mountains," and how Three-fingered Jack had written a statement and drawn a map of the locations. Before he and the gang were surprised by Harry Love's Rangers, he gave the material to "a pious old priest" to be delivered to relatives in Mexico after a certain period. As the Fresno paper told the story, one of Jack's relatives had now appeared in the Coast Range, map in hand. But nobody else ever saw the mysterious stranger.

In April 1890 the *San Francisco Examiner* carried a tale of an Australian lad named David Wall whose father had been killed and robbed by Murieta. Cared for by Joaquin's sweetheart in Monterey, the boy escaped with a treasure map to the gang's booty. He wandered for years on both sides of the border, always pursued and often attacked by members of the band. Finally, at the time of the *Examiner* story, he dug up the treasure chest on Rincon Creek in Santa Barbara County. But of

course no one was around to confirm the story, because Wall —
as the *Examiner* told it — took his treasure and went back to
Australia.

The eagerness of Californians to believe Joaquin treasure
stories was, of course, played upon by schemers and dreamers
alike. In April 1893 (these stories regularly appeared with the
spring thaw) one Felix Sharpers arrived in San Francisco from
Smartsville in the Northern Mines between Marysville and
Grass Valley. With him he carried maps, diagrams and other
documents supposed to show where Murieta's treasure was located in the narrows of the Yuba River above Timbuctoo, near
Smartsville.

Though Joaquin had never been reported in the Northern
Mines, Ridge had credited him with murders near Marysville
and an old legend persisted that a sister of his lived in that
town. So San Francisco merchants subscribed at least $2500
for an expedition that left by train from Oakland to the Northern Mines on April 13. No discovery was ever reported, and
nobody seemed to question why Felix Sharpers, since he had
all the information to find the treasure, needed to share the discovery with others.

But the "will to believe" persisted. In the spring of 1906 an
old man arrived in Mariposa announcing that he had been a
member of Joaquin's gang. By this time the Mariposans had
mellowed, and rather than hanging him out of hand, they
listened. The old man said he was searching for a "secret cave"
high in the cliffs above the Merced River, where Murieta had
buried a large treasure. He was, of course, seeking the help of
prospectors in finding the cave.

The quest he set in motion was pursued by the Mariposans
for 22 years. Then in April 1928 a local prospector named
Manuel Lopez came up with the inevitable "ancient map" to
Joaquin's booty. When he found a cave, the "treasure" consisted of five skeletons.

Meanwhile, in 1911 an old man named Celso Vavoqua
traveled from Fresno to San Francisco with the news that he had
known Joaquin and conversed with him many times; that "Mur-

131

ieta dropped hints as to the hiding place;" that "from subsequent information" he was "now able to locate the exact spot;" and that — sure enough — he was ready to "seek to interest capital to provide funds" for a treasure hunt. But again, no results.

Still the treasure seekers were not discouraged. In 1929 a quest began for a "Murieta cache" near Tailholt, later named White River, as far south as Tulare County. At an "old house with a chimney" in Tailholt, two "mysterious strangers" dug up $20,000 in November 1929, according to the *San Francisco Chronicle*. But, alas, they vanished without identifying themselves, and Californians were once again denied the joy of witnessing a Murieta discovery.

As late as 1942 an expedition was still hunting for Joaquin's treasure — this time near Gilroy in Santa Clara County, where neither the contemporary record nor any of the Joaquin "biographies" ever claimed Murieta had visited. With each passing year the rainbow hunters searched farther from Joaquin's real locale. The quest had deteriorated from the possible to the preposterous.

Still the ultimate in Murieta treasure lore was yet to come. In a 1968 book entitled *Lost Treasures and How to Find Them!*, author Emile C. Schurmacher devoted the opening chapter (10 pages) to Murieta and his buried loot. It is a compound of the Ridge "biography" and other tales. Estimating Joaquin's total treasure cache at from $2 million to $2½ million, the author stated that when the stagecoach operators began melting each gold shipment in a heavy ball to foil Murieta, he began carrying an axe with him to break the gold balls "into large, portable chunks." Some 10 of Murieta's "best authenticated" gold caches were cited in various spots in the Northern Mines. Others were mentioned in Shasta County, Calaveras County, and (between $500,000 and $1,000,000!) in San Diego County.

And why did Joaquin sprinkle California with buried gold? His hauls "were just too heavy and bulky to carry conveniently away in saddlebags."

The contemporary record shows no Joaquin operations in the Northern Mines or Shasta County, no stagecoach holdups anywhere by Murieta or his gang, and a total haul of little more than $21,000 during his two-month public career of banditry.

Hardly less fascinating to Californians were Murieta's alleged hideouts, with or without benefit of treasure. If he had used all of those attributed to him, he would have had no time to commit any crimes.

While no hiding places are cited in the contemporary record, Joaquin was most certainly lying low for two weeks following the battle against Deputy Sheriff Ellas on the hill south of San Andreas on January 23, 1853. He might have hidden in the household of Mexican friends, but at that time most Mexicans were fleeing Calaveras County under Yankee orders. So he could have resorted to a cave on this one occasion, at least.

In February 1906 three boys were exploring Bear Mountain, a ridge some six miles long and ranging up to 2600 feet high, located south of San Andreas and west of Angels Camp. On one of its peaks they climbed a large rock known locally as "Joaquin Murieta's Castle." At the top they rolled off some stones and found a small hole, big enough for eager young boys to enter. Armed with ropes, hatchets and a candle, they lowered themselves into a passageway which, within 50 feet, opened into a fairly large room. There, with mounting excitement, they found a long rusty knife, probably fashioned from a sword. Following another passage they came to a still larger cavern, where they picked up a pair of large-roweled Mexican-style spurs and a one-shot Derringer pistol of the 1850s era. In "high glee," as a Stockton correspondent reported, they returned to the settlements with the news. The *San Francisco Call* announced it with the headlines, "Hiding Place of Bandit is Found by Boys," and "Murietta's Refuge Discovered in Calaveras County."

Whether this was really Joaquin's hideaway could scarcely be verified, but of those linked with his name it is the most likely. Possibly this was the same cave as that located in August 1929 by one D. Fricot, Chairman of the Calaveras County Chamber of Commerce. It was found on the highest point on Bear Mountain, called Carmen Peak. In any case, Fricot announced it as Joaquin's Cave, and that settled the matter for Calaveras County.

Not so elsewhere. Ever since Ridge's biography had emphasized Cantua Canyon as a Murieta headquarters, that remote fastness in western Fresno County was considered hallowed Murieta ground. It was widely understood that the San Joaquin Valley plain near the mouth of Cantua Creek remained a rendezvous of horsethieves after Joaquin's time, as reported in the *San Joaquin Republican* in November 1855. In the early 1880s a woman who advertised herself as the widow of Joaquin Murieta lived in the rocks south of Cantua Creek, where she staged a religious revival for several hundred followers in 1883.

But eight years later the Cantua Canyon area was fairly deserted when two Mexican-Americans dug up, near a spring in a narrow ravine, three skeletons — "one with a bullet hole in the forehead." When this news was brought into Fresno the *San Francisco Chronicle* trumpeted it with the headlines "Probable Victims of Joaquin Murietta," and "Exhumed in a Lonely Region where the Bandit Was Wont to Hide."

As the region was combed by more explorers from Coalinga and Fresno, other identifications were made of Joaquin's hideout. The whole legend was canonized in the U.S. Geological Survey's topographic map of the "Joaquin Rocks Quadrangle," printed in 1943, which identifies a Joaquin Ridge and three pinnacles labeled Joaquin Rocks — not at Cantua Creek, but in the rugged badlands more than five miles south.

Despite all this, there is no contemporary evidence that Joaquin ever used Cantua Creek or any other locality as a hiding place or rendezvous. When Harry Love's California Rangers killed the four Mexicans they claimed were Murieta and his gang, their victims had been camping on the floor of the San Joaquin Valley near the mouth of Cantua Creek — not in the hills. Ridge's "biography" is, of course, laden with conversations between Joaquin, his sweetheart and his men at a "Cantoova Creek" rendezvous, and it is from this fancy that the "Joaquin Rocks" legend sprang.

Still other Joaquin haunts and hideouts needed no source at all to become legend. Any interesting cave or unusual rock formation seemed enough to convince California imaginations that Joaquin "used to hide there." One such labyrinth, located in Pinnacles National Monument, has been solemnly posted as a Murieta hideout with no apparent justification other than being located merely 40 miles across a mountain range from Cantua Creek. In 1893 the *Sacramento Union* described a cave in Yuba County, 50 miles above Joaquin's northernmost foray, as a Murieta hideaway. A huge domerock in the Deer Creek region of Tulare County, more than 130 miles below Joaquin's southernmost escapade in Mariposa County, was settled upon as a Murieta hangout. As the *San Francisco Chronicle's* correspondent wrote in 1929: "Old-timers say Murietta's 'ghost' can be seen around the rock at certain hours of the night."

With this kind of competition, the Mother Lode towns that could legitimately claim a visitation by Joaquin began looking to their landmarks.

Mokelumne Hill claimed it was at the Zumwalt Saloon (no longer standing) that Joaquin performed one of the feats attributed to him by Ridge — that of challenging a miner who had boasted of killing Murieta on sight. Fiddletown came up with its own version of the same story.

San Andreas claimed to be the locale of the "episode" in which Joaquin bought a coat of chain mail for $1000 from a Frenchman and when it arrived from Europe, made the Frenchman put it on while he emptied his revolver into it. Since the Frenchman was unscratched, Joaquin bought the armor — thus explaining why he was able to make so many escapes unharmed by gunfire.

Finally, the town of Hornitos displays a sign showing the tunnel through which Joaquin "used to" escape from a fandango hall whenever he was discovered. Escape in Hornitos he did, but not from a fandango hall and not by a tunnel.

Other and more general claims were made for Joaquin sojourns in other towns — Murphy's, Vallecito, Calaveritas, and Angel's Camp in Calaveras County; Sonora, Jamestown, and

Sawmill Flat in Tuolumne County; Placerville, Marysville, New Idria, San Jose, and Monterey.

That so many towns lay proprietary claim to Joaquin is a tribute not to that miserable cutthroat, but to the romantic heart of California. Peeled to the core, Joaquin was the vicious slayer of helpless Chinese. It is not this, but a make-believe Joaquin who lives in the lore of California towns. Such accumulated Joaquin mythology was appropriately measured in 1936 by columnist Earl Ennis in the *San Francisco Chronicle:*

"According to my grandfather Joaquin Murietta was always going about the country doing kind deeds. Once he shot a whole company of infantry because they marched through an old lady's cornfield."

CHAPTER FIFTEEN

The Myth Killers

THE MYTHICAL JOAQUIN, created by the "biographers" and nurtured by local pride, could not live forever.
But surprisingly, his attackers were not professional historians
who could have gone behind Ridge to the original sources. Instead they were alert literary detectives who peeled off the accretions of pirated "Lives" to the original Ridge.

At first, 20th Century bibliographers could scarcely find the
earliest "biographies." Rare copies of the 1871 Ridge edition
were available, but the original 1854 version was more a myth
than Joaquin himself. The Library of Congress had a set of the
1859 *California Police Gazettes* which serialized the second
Joaquin "Life," but the booklet reprint which fathered and
grandfathered so many other "Lives" was also missing.

Some time before 1932 the *Police Gazette* booklet turned up in San Francisco. It was republished with an introduction by Francis P. Farquhar, a noted San Francisco accountant who was perhaps better known as an accomplished geographer, explorer, conservationist, and bibliographer.

Farquhar presented the *Police Gazette* "Life" not so much as history as "an entertaining story." He noted the differences between this "Carmela-Clarina" version and "the prototype of the 'Rosita' version" — Ridge. But since the supposed 1854 Ridge edition was still undiscovered, Farquhar insisted that "the question of plagiarism cannot be conclusively settled." He did show how subsequent versions both in English and Spanish were pirated from the *Police Gazette* version.

As for the real Murieta, Farquhar conceded "that there was such a person, that he was the leader of a very active band of murderers and robbers, and that he occasionally indulged in acts of startling bravado." But Joaquin's "spectacular death" and the public showing of his "pickled visage" stimulated "all manner of tales of his exploits:"

> Chivalry and gallantry became his attributes; his dark deeds took the shape of vengeance for wrongs committed against him and his lovely wife . . . in short, he became a fabulous character.

Up to this point the attack on the Murieta legend was on solid ground. While sidestepping any historical research, it did not challenge Joaquin's existence and confined itself to assaulting the legend. In fact, even Farquhar accepted too much of the Murieta story — that his reign of terror lasted two years, that his gang included "Three-fingered Jack," and that "with the annihilation of these leaders this particular type of banditry promptly subsided."

Appearing shortly after the publication of Walter Noble Burns' *The Robin Hood of El Dorado,* Farquhar's 1932 study seemed but a "voice crying in the wilderness" of Murieta fantasy. But in 1937 a copy of the original 1854 Ridge version turned up, enabling literary scholar Franklin D. Walker to compare it with the 1871 Ridge edition. In his study for the *Cali-*

fornia Historical Society Quarterly, Walker declared unequivocally that Ridge had been plagiarized and that "the *Police Gazette* version is based upon Ridge's account . . ." He also suggested that the 1854 Ridge book "did more to fix the outline of the legend than any actual events in social history," since "the evidence in newspapers and military records concerning Joaquin is both meager and contradictory."

Pursuing this line of inquiry in his *San Francisco's Literary Frontier* (1939), Walker devoted 10 pages to Ridge's own life as a Cherokee fugitive and California newspaperman, showing how the author's own psychological tensions — hatred of oppressors, desire for revenge — had been unleashed in the pages of *Joaquin*. Ridge had even noted the face of each of his own father's assassins, had learned their names, and had admitted "a deep-seated principle of Revenge . . . which will never be satisfied, until it reaches its object."

From this pent-up rancor Ridge ejected the tale of Joaquin's suffering and vengeance. "Thus," as Walker concluded, "the massacre of an Indian on the Cherokee reserve colored the most vital of Western folk-tales."

Taking up Joaquin himself, Walker called him "a petty brigand little more romantic than the countless other bandits of Latin-American societies." He correctly confined Joaquin's public career to "the spring of 1853" and reported that his gang "exterminated Chinese like coveys of quail . . ." Walker cast doubt on the head brought back by the rangers by derogating its sponsors. Harry Love was a "vicious" adventurer and his rangers "as disreputable a group of thugs as ever killed under the law." In fact, it was probably due to "the notoriety of the Love gang and the exhibition of the pickled head" that Joaquin rose in legend above his contemporaries in crime.

Exposure of the Joaquin myth was now in full cry, though in danger of following a false lead by prematurely dismissing the real Joaquin.

At this point the trail was picked up by a still more persistent literary sleuth, Joseph Henry Jackson — author, bibliophile, crime authority, and book editor of the *San Francisco Chroni-*

cle. In 1941 Jackson devoted 11 pages to Joaquin Murieta in his valuable book on the California Gold Rush and the Mother Lode Country, *Anybody's Gold.* Reasserting Farquhar's chronicle of the "piratings of piratings" back to the original Joaquin biographies, Jackson added the further point that even in 1853 the *Alta California* had doubted Love's encounter with the true Joaquin and declared his Joaquin head a "humbug." So far as Murieta himself was concerned, "the known facts are few and the inventions are many."

Jackson was not yet ready to say that the first Murieta did not exist. In fact, he accepted the belief that Three-fingered Jack — "a villain of the deepest dye"—was Murieta's "right-hand man." It was only that "nobody knows very much about" Murieta.

But Jackson was fascinated with the Murieta mystery. The deeper he dug — still confining himself to sources published after Joaquin's career had closed — the more he was convinced that the invention of Joaquin included not only the legend and the head, but even the man himself.

In 1948 he wrote an article for the *Pacific Spectator* entitled "The Creation of Joaquin Murieta." In it he claimed that "John Rollin Ridge, in his preposterous little book, actually created both the man, Murieta, and the Murieta legend." Californians needed a hero, and "since there wasn't a Murieta — at any rate not much of a Murieta — it was necessary to create one."

The next year Joe Jackson expanded on this theme with a 38-page chapter in his entertaining book on California highwaymen, *Bad Company.* He provided a thoroughgoing recount of all the Murieta tales since Ridge — "biographies," romances, poems, dramas and magazine articles, in English and Spanish — an exhaustive hunt well beyond Farquhar in the thickets of Joaquin literature. He concluded that Ridge had manufactured Joaquin Murieta "practically out of whole cloth . . ."

By this time Joseph Henry Jackson was the accepted authority on Murieta, or rather, non-Murieta. When the original Ridge 1854 edition was republished in 1955, Jackson wrote an introduction which was unique in denying the truth of that which it introduced.

Gone now was California's cherished bandit hero. The myth-makers, from Ridge to Burns, were exposed. Bancroft and Hittell were chastised and corrected at last.

Only in the Spanish language did the old Joaquin persist. In Santiago, Chile, Pablo Neruda wrote another drama about "Joaquin Murieta, Bandido Chileno," as late as 1967.

But history-wise Californians knew better. The life and death of their Joaquin is epitomized in the works of the distinguished 20th Century California historian, Robert Glass Cleland. As late as 1944 he was writing that "Murieta and his lieutenant, the sadistic 'Three-fingered Jack,' terrorized the state from 1851 to 1853." But by 1951 he dismissed Murieta as "half-mythical."

The pendulum of historical fashion had swung from one extreme to the other. After having too much Joaquin, California now had none. Conscientious literary detectives had done the historians' work for them in burying the false Joaquin. But more than a century after the facts, nobody had yet dug for the real one.

CHAPTER SIXTEEN

Joaquin: The Man Behind the Myth

THE HISTORY of California's most famous bandit has os-
cillated between two contradictions — that he ravaged the
state for two years as an epic Robin Hood figure, and that he
amounted to little or nothing. One cannot believe both, and in
fact, one should not believe either.

Oddly ignored for more than a century, first-hand accounts

*Left: The stone-walled jail still stood at Hornitos in the 1970s
as a reminder of the roaring days of a century before.*

tell of a bandit named Joaquin who cut a wide swath across California's gold country. At least three rewards from different sources were posted for his head. He and his band killed at least 24 and probably 29 people. Half-a-dozen posses rode after them at one time or another. Sixteen Mexicans or native Californians were shot or lynched because they were thought to belong to Joaquin's band.

The placers were so terrorized by Joaquin's butchery that settlers fled the mines in droves. And so aroused was the mining population that the state of California sent out a special force of rangers to end the depredations.

This was no penny-ante pirate. Joaquin was a dead shot, a superb horseman, daring in his appearances and astonishing in his escapes. He tried to steal his pursuers' own horses, he murdered while his pursuers were within earshot, he robbed while they were in sight!

So much for the Joaquin that was. There also are many things that he was not:

1. *The bearer of many aliases.* During his bandit career in the gold fields he was known only as Joaquin. A reward notice of February 21, 1853, gave his last name as Carillo. This never took hold in the public press, and after his bandit career was over he began to be called Joaquin Muriati, Muliatta, and finally Murieta. This was the name of a horse thief who had operated in Southern California. Whether the two were the same is possible but not provable.

2. *The romantic avenger.* There is no first-hand evidence of any raping-lynching-whipping episode that drove Joaquin to a life of crime. True, several of his associates were lynched by American mobs, and more than once he resumed his pillage immediately after. But these events occurred after he had launched his bandit career, and in any case his victims were usually Chinese, who had not wronged him. According to one account, the brother of the bandit Joaquin was lynched in San Andreas in February 1853. But again, this was well after Joaquin's bloody career had begun. Another, possibly a nephew of Murieta the horsethief, was lynched in Los Angeles in 1852,

but this was at least a year after Murieta had begun stealing livestock.

3. *A Robin Hood outlaw — defending the oppressed, sharing with the poor.* Of the 24 victims reported killed by Joaquin and his band as they swept through the Southern Mines, 19 were Chinese — who shared with Mexicans the oppression of the *Americanos,* were notably inoffensive, and seldom armed. There is no contemporary record that Joaquin ever performed a kindness for any of his fellow countrymen. There is one report that Joaquin Murieta the horsethief stole 30 animals from one of his *compadres,* and another that the Joaquin of the placers attacked a Mexican-American family in San Diego County as he was heading for the border.

4. *The guerrilla chieftain, with hundreds at his command.* Joaquin was nothing more than a bandit, improvising his crimes as he went along. There is no evidence that he planned any rebellion in California or that he had a latent organization ready to spring up in revolt. The most he ever mustered was 11 men in the fight on the hill south of San Andreas late in January 1853. As he lost men he recruited others, but he usually had no more than three or four followers at a time.

5. *A miraculous gadfly who seemed to strike at several widely scattered places at once.* The contemporary record shows a clear-cut chronology of Joaquin appearances in his bandit career. Only toward the end of his apparent flight to Mexico were there conflicting reports of his whereabouts, and these were more in the nature of rumors.

6. *The terror of California from 1851 to 1853.* The evidence shows that one Joaquin Murieta was a horsethief known only in Los Angeles from late 1851 to late 1852. The bandit Joaquin operated only in Calaveras County (including the part which soon after became Amador County), the lower edge of El Dorado County, and probably in Mariposa County. This period in which the name Joaquin was associated with crimes reported in the public press lasted from January 26 to March 18, 1853 — less than two months. There is no evidence that he was connected with various crimes attributed to him in other parts

of the state at other times — the murder of General Bean of Los Angeles County, Sheriff Clark of Santa Clara County, or Sheriff Wilson of Santa Barbara County, or the wounding of Sheriff Buchanan in Yuba County.

7. *The commander of confederates who had horses waiting for him in relays to effect his escapes.* Joaquin was a master of impromptu disappearances. He stole the horses he needed to escape, usually picking the best horseflesh in sight.

8. *The companion of Three-fingered Jack.* The first mention of Three-fingered Jack in the contemporary record is after the supposed slaying of Joaquin at Cantua Creek. A "Four-fingered Jack" was a California character as early as the Mexican War, 1846-7, but there is no evidence that this is the same man shot by Love and his men at Cantua Creek. All of the Three-fingered Jack episodes in the Murieta "biographies" are inventions.

9. *The lover of Rosita, Clarita, Carmela, Carmen, etc.* Except for Ana Benitez, the woman of Joaquin Murieta the horse-thief in Los Angeles, no woman was linked with Joaquin in the contemporary record. The Rosita, Carmela, etc. episodes are all fiction.

10. *The user of haunts and hideouts identified throughout California.* No first-hand evidence links Joaquin with any cave, tunnel, canyon, building or other physical object anywhere in California. The only towns whose claims of a Joaquin visit are supported by contemporary evidence are Los Angeles, San Andreas, Lancha Plana, Campo Seco, Jackson Gate, Drytown, Fiddletown, Quartzburg, and Hornitos.

11. *The planter of treasure troves throughout California.* There is no evidence that Joaquin or his gang ever buried any loot anywhere in California.

12. *The victim and the trophy of Harry Love and the California Rangers.* From the record, Harry Love's claim is very difficult to credit, and it is more likely that he brought back the head of another person.

Finally, there are some fragments of the Joaquin pattern that may never be known for certain. From what origins did he spring in Mexico? What crimes if any did he commit before he became publicly identified as Joaquin? Did he really have brothers or sisters living in various California towns? Did he remain in hiding or incognito in California, or did he get away to Mexico? If the latter, how did he spend his remaining years? As a successful ranchero in Sonora, as a public official under an assumed name in Peru, or as one of the other improbable characters described in later stories? Or did he take refuge in merciful obscurity, imparting blood-dyed recollections to some latter-day Rosita? *Quien sabe?*

Bibliography

PUBLIC RECORDS
(California State Archives)

Petition, citizens of Mariposa County to the California Legislature, for a company of 20 or 25 California Rangers, Mariposa County, April 20, 1853.

Petition, residents of Mariposa County to Governor John Bigler, for at least 20 California Rangers to be headed by Captain Harry Love, Mariposa County, 1853.

By the late twentieth century, Joaquin Murieta's name was part of the legendary West. This illustration humorously depicting Joaquin was used in an advertisement by the San Francisco Chronicle.

149

Report of Select Committee composed of the Tuolumne Delegates on the Bill referred to them to create a Sabbath day in that County . . ., Benicia, 1853.

Journal of the Fourth Session of the Legislature of the State of California, San Francisco, 1853. March 28, 30, April 14, May 10, 11, 12, 14, 16, 17, 1853, and Appendix No. 49.

Journal of the Fifth Session of the Legislature of the State of California, San Francisco, 1854. April 28, May 1, 9, 13, 15, 1854.

Letter, Harry Love to Governor John Bigler, San Juan Bautista, Calif., July 12, 1853.

Letter, Harry Love to Governor John Bigler, Quartzburg, August 4, 1853.

Muster and Descriptive Roll of Captain Harry Love's Company of California State Rangers for the month ending July 28, 1853.

Statement concerning prisoner Jose Maria Ochova, by J. Boling, Sheriff; E. Burke, District Attorney; and 16 others, Mariposa County, August 5, 1853.

Affidavits on the authenticity of the head claimed to be that of Joaquin Murieta:

> John Green, Quartzburg, Mariposa County, August 7, 1853
>
> Henry C. Long, Quartzburg, Mariposa County, August 7, 1853
>
> Pedro Montea, Quartzburg, Mariposa County, August 7, 1853
>
> Jose Maria Vaga, Quartzburg, Mariposa County, August 7, 1853

Affidavits, cont'd

> Stephen Bond, Quartzburg, Mariposa County, August 8, 1853
>
> Susan Banta, Quartzburg, Mariposa County, August 8, 1853
>
> Juliet G. Thorp, Quartzburg, Mariposa County, August 8, 1853
>
> William Byrnes (Burns), Quartzburg, Mariposa County, August 8, 1853
>
> Henry V. McCargar, San Joaquin County, August 11, 1853
>
> Rev. Father Dominic Baine, San Joaquin County, August 11, 1853
>
> Dr. N. B. Hubbell, Stockton, San Joaquin County, August 12, 1853
>
> Clemente Morales
> Jose Maria Rivera
> Bernardo Reyna   } Stockton, San Joaquin County,
> Francisco Revarro   August 12, 1853
> G. W. Havens

Certification of Harry Love "that Joaquin could not have been taken alive," and was "shot on my order." Benicia, August 27, 1853.

Statement of Governor John Bigler certifying that Harry Love is "entitled to the reward of $1000 . . ." Benicia, August 27, 1853.

Comptroller's Warrant No. 362, August 29, 1853, Treasurer of State to Harry Love, $1000 "for capturing Joaquin."

NEWSPAPERS

(Bancroft Library, Henry E. Huntington Library and
Art Gallery, California State Library, Los Angeles
Public Library, San Diego Public Library, Stanford
University Library, Stockton Public Library,
U.C.L.A. Research Library, and Library of Congress)

Auburn *Weekly Placer Herald,* Feb. 5, 26, March 5, 19, April
2, May 21, June 11, July 23, Aug. 6, 13, 20, 1853.

Calaveras Chronicle, March 19, 1853.

Columbia Gazette (Collection of Donald Segerstrom, Sonora,
Calif.), Feb. 12, 19, 26, March 5, 1853.

Fresno Expositor, Nov. 12, 1879 (Reminiscence of William
Henderson)

Los Angeles Star, May 17, July 12, 1851; June 19, 26, Nov. 13,
27, 1852; March 12, June 4, 11, 18, July 16, Aug. 6, Sept.
3, 1853.

New York Herald, June 28, 1849.

Sacramento Union, Nov. 12, 13, 14, 15, 18, 19, 20, 1851; Jan.
31, Feb. 14, 15, 18, 19, 22, 24, March 18, 22, 24, 29, 31,
April 23, May 6, 10, June 8, 18, July 30, Aug. 9, 11, 13,
15, 25, 26, 1853.

Sacramento Bee, Oct. 7, 1867.

San Diego Herald, March 19, 1853.

San Francisco *Alta California,* Dec. 15, 18, 1852; Jan. 29,
Feb. 14, 16, 18, 21, 24, March 4, 16, July 3, 15, 30, 31, Au-
gust 1, 2, 4, 5, 7, 10, 12, 13, 16, 18, 23, Sept. 1, 1853;
April 30, July 3, 1854; March 24, 28, April 13, 1855; June
7, Sept. 18, Oct. 5, 1856; July 29, 1857; June 18, 1858;
Feb. 10, 1863; Oct. 8, 1867; July 2, 1868; April 2, 1873;
Nov. 10, 1879.

San Francisco Call, Dec. 29, 1882; April 14, July 20, 1883;
Oct. 20, 1885; Oct. 14, 1887; April 3, 1892; April 12, 28,
Nov. 5, 1893; Feb. 20, 1906; Feb. 4, 1911.

San Francisco Chronicle, (Steamer edition); August 16, 1854;
Dec. 20, 1891; Oct. 3, 1909; June 19, 1927; April 8, 9,
1928; Aug. 9, 28, Nov. 30, 1929; Dec. 19, 1931; April 17,
1936; Nov. 17, 1942.

San Francisco Examiner, April 6, 1890; Dec. 17, 1893; May 29, 1921; Jan. 6, 1924.

San Francisco Herald, April 4, 18, 29, May 9, Aug. 19, 20, 1853.

San Francisco *Pacific,* July 29, August 19, 1853.

San Francisco *Sun,* July 25, 1853.

San Jose Pioneer, Nov. 29, 1879.

Stockton *San Joaquin Republican,* Jan. 26, 29, Feb. 2, 16, 19, 23, 26, March 2, 9, 12, 16, 30, April 23, 30, May 4, 18, 28, June 8, 21, July 12, 16, 26, 30, Aug. 2, 6, 11, 1853.

PERIODICALS

California Police Gazette, Vol. 1, No. 2, July 16, 1854 (Chapters III and IV of "Joaquin, the Mountain Robber; or the Guerrilla of California").

California Police Gazette, Vol. 1, Nos. 34-43, Sept. 3 to Nov. 5, 1859 ("The Life of Joaquin Murieta, The Brigand Chief of California").

Gordon, David E., "Early California Journalism: John Rollin Ridge," *Overland,* Aug. 1904.

Jackson, Joseph Henry, "The Creation of Joaquin Murieta," *The Pacific Spectator,* Spring 1948.

Latta, Frank, "Murrieta Rides Again," *The Pony Express,* July, August, September, 1962; March, June, 1963; January 1964.

Nadeau, Remi, "Joaquin — Hero, Villain or Myth?" *Westways,* Jan. 1963.

——————— and Nadeau, Margaret, "Joaquin — Dead or Alive?" *Westways,* Aug. 1970.

Walker, Franklin D., "Ridge's Life of Joaquin Murieta: The First and Revised Editions Compared," *California Historical Society Quarterly,* September 1937.

———————, "Yellow Bird," *Westways,* Nov. 1938.

Wood, Raymund F., "New Light on Joaquin Murrieta," *Pacific Historian,* Winter 1970.

PUBLISHED WORKS

Alley, Bowen & Co., pub., *History of Santa Clara County, California,* San Francisco, 1881.

Badger, Joseph E., Jr., *Joaquin, The Saddle King,* New York, 1881 (fiction).

————, *Joaquin, the Terrible,* New York, 1881.

Bancroft, Hubert Howe, *California Pastoral,* San Francisco, 1888.

————, *History of California,* Vol. 7, San Francisco, 1890.

Bell, Maj. Horace, *Reminiscences of a Ranger,* Los Angeles, 1881.

————, *On the Old West Coast,* New York, 1930.

Burns, Walter Noble, *The Robin Hood of El Dorado,* New York, 1932.

California Police Gazette, pub., *Joaquin Murieta: The Brigand Chief of California,* San Francisco, 1859. Reprinted, with an introduction by Francis P. Farquhar, San Francisco, 1932.

Chalfant, W. A., *The Story of Inyo,* Chicago, 1922.

Coolidge, Dane, *Gringo Gold; a Story of Joaquin Murieta, the Bandit.* New York, 1939 (fiction).

Cossley- Batt, Jill L., *The Last of the California Rangers,* New York, 1928 (a biography drawn from reminiscences of William J. Howard, member of the California Rangers).

Cunningham, J. C., *The Truth about Murietta,* Los Angeles, 1938.

Hayes, Judge Benjamin I., *Pioneer Notes from the Diaries of Judge Benjamin Hayes,* Los Angeles, 1929 (Ed. by Marjorie Tisdale Wolcott).

Hernandez, A. Acevedo, *Joaquin Murieta; drama en seis actos,* Santiago de Chile, 1936.

Herrero, Ignacio, *Joaquin Murrieta, el Bandido Chileno en California,* San Antonio, Texas, 1926.

Hittell, Theodore, *History of California,* Vol. 3, San Francisco, 1897.

Howe, Charles E. B., *A Dramatic Play Entitled Joaquin Murieta de Castillo, the Celebrated Bandit,* San Francisco, 1858.

154

Hyenne, Roberto, *El Bandido Chileno, Joaquin Murieta en California,* Santiago, Chile, 1906. Illustrated Edition, Barcelona and Mexico City, n.d.

Jackson, Joseph Henry, *Anybody's Gold,* New York, 1941.

—————, *Bad Company,* New York, 1949.

Klette, Ernest, *The Crimson Trail of Joaquin Murieta,* Los Angeles, 1928.

Mason, J. D. (Thompson & West, pub.), *History of Amador County, California,* Oakland, 1881.

Nadeau, Remi, *Ghost Towns and Mining Camps of California,* Los Angeles, 1965.

Neruda, Pablo, *Fulgor y Muerte de Joaquin Murieta, Bandido Chileno . . .,* Santiago de Chile, 1967 (a drama).

Paz, Ireneo, *Vida y Aventuras del mas Celebre Bandido Sonorense Joaquin Murrieta,* Mexico City, 1908.

—————, *Life and Adventures of the Celebrated Bandit Joaquin Murrieta,* Trans. by Francis P. Belle, Chicago, 1925.

Peeples, Samuel Anthony, *The Dream Ends in Fury, a Novel Based on the Life of Joaquin Murrieta,* New York, 1949.

Ridge, John Rollin ("Yellow Bird"), *Life and Adventures of Joaquin Murieta, the Celebrated California Bandit,* San Francisco, 1854. Reprinted, with an introduction by Joseph Henry Jackson, Norman, Okla., 1955.

—————, *Life and Adventures of Joaquin Murieta, the Brigand Chief of California,* New Edition, with "much new and heretofore unpublished material," San Francisco, 1871. Reprinted, Hollister, Calif., 1927.

Sargent, Mrs. J. L. (ed), *Amador County History,* Jackson, Calif., 1927.

Secrest, William B., *Joaquin,* Fresno, 1967.

Stewart, Marcus A., *Rosita: a California Tale,* San Jose, Calif., 1882.

Walker, Franklin D., *San Francisco's Literary Frontier,* New York, 1939.

Wood, Richard Coke, *Tales of Old Calaveras,* Angels Camp, Calif., 1949.

————, *Calaveras, the Land of Skulls,* Sonora, Calif., 1955.

Wood, Raymund F., *Mariana LaLoca: "Prophetess of the Cantua" and Alleged Spouse of Joaquin Murrieta,* Fresno, Calif., 1970.

MISCELLANEOUS

Davis, Winfield, Scrapbook of Clippings (Henry E. Huntington Library and Art Gallery).

Hayes, Judge Benjamin I., Scrapbooks, Vols. 11 and 43 (Bancroft Library).

Poster advertising exhibition of "The Head of the renowned Bandit! Joaquin! and the Hand of Three Fingered Jack," Stockton House, August 12, 1853.

Walkup, W. B., "Official Map of Calaveras County," 1895.

Wood, N. T., "Reminiscences of Early Days in California." Manuscript in Henry E. Huntington Library and Art Gallery.

Index

Italics indicate references to the titles of books and motion pictures and the names of periodicals. Numbers in parenthesis refer to illustrations.